Interracial Public Housing
in Border City

Interracial Public Housing in Border City

A Situational Analysis of
The Contact Hypothesis

W. Scott Ford
The Florida State University

Lexington Books
D. C. Heath and Company
Lexington, Massachusetts
Toronto   London

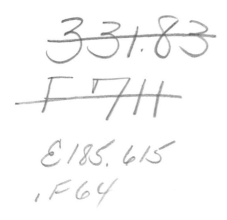

Library of Congress Cataloging in Publication Data

Ford, W. Scott.
 Interracial public housing in Border City.

 Includes bibliographical references.
  1. United States – Race question. 2. Public housing – United States.
I. Title.
El85.615.F64   301.5'4   75-39896
ISBN 0-669-83246-4

Published simultaneously in Canada.

Printed in the United States of America.

International Standard Book Number: 0-669-83246-4

Library of Congress Catalog Card Number: 75-39896

For My Parents

The world of prejudice, it would appear, is a world of false fears leading to real sorrows.

Robert M. MacIver

Contents

List of Tables

Acknowledgements

Many colleagues and members of the Border City community lent their time, skills, and encouragement to the research effort reported in this monograph. Discussion with Joseph W. Scott and Harry K. Schwarzweller provided useful insight in the design of the research. I appreciate the critical comments of A. Lee Coleman who read an earlier draft of the manuscript. I am especially grateful to Willis A. Sutton, Jr., who spent considerable time reading early drafts and offered thoughtful criticism and suggestions for revision.

Appreciation is due to Gregory Shinert who made it possible to gather the required sampling data. Anne Washington and Gervita Flynn proved to be perceptive informants as well as accomplished interviewers. Special appreciation goes to my wife, Ann, for her help in coding the interview data and most importantly for her continued encouragement throughout the various stages of research and writing. I gratefully acknowledge the cooperation of the public housing residents who allowed us access to their homes and permitted themselves to be interviewed at length.

Several persons at the Florida State University were particularly helpful in the preparation of the manuscript. Among them, Charles M. Grigg, director of the Institute for Social Research, provided the author with his continued encouragement and support. Dru Geissal made the task of completing the monograph easier by her work as my graduate assistant. My thanks are also extended to Carolyn Evans who typed the manuscript. Of course, I willingly accept the responsibility for the interpretations contained within the study.

Interracial Public Housing
in Border City

1

The Contact Hypothesis

Another Interracial Contact Study?

In the two decades between the close of World War II and the Watts Riot in Los Angeles an impressive body of social science research was published which indicated that when blacks and whites regularly associated with one another under favorable circumstances, and *as social equals*, there resulted a reduction of racial intolerance. The testing of this "contact hypothesis" largely grew out of the wartime research of Stouffer and his associates who studied interracial attitudes among servicemen.[1] Subsequently, the two contact situations most frequently investigated were place of work and residence. The research reported in this monograph fits best with other studies of race and residence. However, it was not solely designed as a replication study of the contact hypothesis. It was, as will be explained, purposely designed to avoid some of the shortcomings of earlier studies.

In the years since Watts — years characterized by dramatic urban racial unrest — there have been few sociological studies of the effects of interpersonal interracial contact. It appears that the publication of Robin Williams' well known *Stranger Next Door* signaled the end of a period of considerable interest in this issue.[2] It is likely that one or both of the following related assumptions have been responsible for the lack of current interest in contact studies: (1) By the middle of the last decade, we had learned all there was to learn about the effects of interpersonal equal-status contacts between blacks and whites; a relatively large number of studies, conducted by different researchers in a variety of research settings, generally corroborated the contact hypothesis. (2) Ghetto riots, heated racial confrontations and the fiery rhetoric of black militants all minimized the likelihood of interpersonal contacts between the races taking place or assured that they would be particularly guarded when they occurred. Therefore, it would be increasingly difficult to isolate and study circumstances wherein the effects of interracial contacts could be observed.

It is encouraging that much of the sociological research in the field of race has refocused its attentions upon macrostructural concerns and moved away from the previous dominance of attitudinal studies. However, to the extent that the above assumptions are responsible for a total abandonment of contact studies, we labor under faulty assumptions and seriously neglect an important research

3

issue. Whereas we should rigorously support and emphasize studies of institutionalized racism, collective behavior, and urban policy evaluations, we should not lose sight of the fact that there remains a necessity for examining the effects of interracial contact. Such study is essential for a fuller understanding of American race relations, and moreover, this research is still feasible. We do not know all there is to know; this is particularly true of the black response to interpersonal situations said to be "equal-status" in nature. We underestimate the number of opportunities that exist whereby we can observe blacks and whites relating to one another under circumstances which approach equal-status conditions. Although the author concurs with the "action-oriented" who argue that a "change-the-situation" ("system") approach should take precedence over a "change-the-person" ("attitude") strategy in the fight against racial inequality, this does not negate the importance of looking at the effects of interracial contact in the post-Watts United States. In short, it is precisely because "the times have changed" that it remains important to reexamine the contact hypothesis.

The major focus of the field study reported herein is a reexamination of the contact or interaction hypothesis. The assertion that equal-status contact is positively related to racial tolerance is retested by examining interracial neighboring and a series of other equal-status situations as they relate to the racial attitudes and perceptions of black and white public housing residents in a border state city. That this research makes a genuine, if modest, contribution is largely due to three factors: (1) the contact hypothesis was examined within a socioenvironmental setting not yet investigated; (2) an equal and overdue emphasis is given to black reactions to contact with whites; and (3) blacks and whites, sharing the same socioeconomic lifestyle, were asked to react to residential desegregation — a process which they were experiencing first hand.

At the time of the field work (summer, 1967) the racial characteristics and location of municipal housing projects in Border City[a] made it possible to interview women of each race in three distinct project environments: in racially segregated projects; in projects predominantly occupied by families of the other race; and in a fully desegregated project. Research hypotheses, formulated prior to the field work, were tested using interview data. A more detailed description of the research setting and the data collection are presented in chapter 2. Before turning to a brief discussion of contact studies, which provide the theoretical framework for the present research, let us pause and consider what is meant by equal-status interracial contact.

What Is "Equal-Status" Contact?

Equal-status contacts have been defined as interracial relationships that "involve

---

[a]Border City is a pseudonym. The city is described in some detail in chapter 2.

an active ... personal approach ... on a basis of implied social equality."[3] In other words, these are relatively sustained interpersonal contacts within situations wherein no party is defined or considered subordinate. Such contacts, however, are not autonomous events unaffected by other social circumstances. Their effects are circumscribed by the preexisting attitudes of the participants and various social forces which may qualify the hypothesized relationship between contact and attitude change spelled out above. Methodologically, the concept remains somewhat elusive. A genuine problem arises when we attempt to determine which interpersonal contacts between individuals of different races are equalitarian in nature. This becomes especially difficult if we require that such contacts be similarly or identically interpreted by both black and white. Although this is essentially a problem of measurement, Simpson and Yinger have suggested that differential interpretations of contact can lead to inconclusive evidence concerning the affects of contact upon racial prejudice.[4] This suggestion has never been seriously pursued. We will return to this issue when interpreting the results of the present research.

Beyond the problems of measurement, it should be recognized that by choosing equal-status contact as an explanatory variable, we literally refer to a type of interpersonal contact that is infrequently found! Contact between black and white Americans has long taken place within institutionalized settings wherein blacks play subordinate roles. Because of these prevalent status differentials, any relationship between black and white, even between persons of the same socioeconomic class, may be readily perceived as one of inequality. Social forces operate upon members of both racial groups so that seldom are any interracial contacts experiences except those which reflect dominant-subordinate relationships. The traditional restrictions which prevent the two races from engaging in truly equal-status relationships have frequently been documented and need not be elaborated here.[5]

In view of the perpetuation of vestiges of caste-like relationships, equal-status contacts might better be interpreted as those interpersonal contacts that approach or suggest a situation of social equality. Undoubtedly more important than any "objective" appraisal of an interracial contact situation is the respective participants' "definition of the situation." If an individual who relates to a member of the other race interprets this relationship as one which implies social equality, then the consequences of this contact are as real for him as if "objective" equality actually existed. Nonetheless, continued status inequality between the races does not render the contact hypothesis untenable. In fact, it is because such equal-status interracial experiences are uncommon that their occurrence brings about a change in attitude and perception on the part of the persons involved.

A Basic Theoretical Assumption

In a rudimentary sense, the contact hypothesis states a theory of attitude and behavior change. It suggests that whenever members of different racial or ethnic groups regularly associate with one another under favorable circumstances, and as social equals, the result is a reduction of intergroup prejudice and discrimination. This theoretical perspective is an outgrowth of several decades of social research in the area of ethnic and racial prejudice and has been discussed at length by Williams as well as a number of other writers;[6] a recent summary of evidence is presented by Pettigrew.[7] This perspective of intergroup relations closely approximates that which Allport has called the "situational" approach;[8] equal-status contact is viewed as a situational determinant of racial tolerance. The assumption is made that individuals' feelings and views concerning race are products of social relations. The rationale for treating behavioral factors as independent variables is found throughout the literature on race relations. For example, while cautioning that the assumption of one-way influence is an oversimplification, Raab and Lipset conclude that available evidence indicates that attitudes ultimately shape themselves to behavior and not the reverse.[9] Attitudes rarely change without a preceding change in the behavioral circumstances in which people find themselves. Interracial antipathy increases or decreases as a product of such preceding changes.

The primary reason for emphasizing equal-status contacts is that these contacts reduce stereotyped images. Arnold Rose argued that when racial prejudice is seen as an emotionally charged attitude directed toward a stereotyped object, a weakening of that stereotype will result in a corresponding reduction of prejudice.[10] Racial stereotypes can condition behavior patterns between group members, and subsequent subordinate behavior of a minority perpetuates the stereotype. When equal-status contacts are employed as explanations of reduced racial prejudice, they are essentially viewed as an initial step in interrupting this "vicious circle."[11] It is argued that social equality in interracial contact allows persons to react to one another on a basis of perceived individual qualities rather than as members of social categories. Westie contends that racial stereotypes are frequently held by persons who have had little or no direct contact with minority group members.[12] Stereotypes seldom arise directly from interpersonal contact; they generally stem from the normative order which prescribes appropriate behavior toward out-group members.[13] Even among those who are initially intolerant and who have strongly resisted intergroup contact, equal-status contacts generally have reduced prejudice. In fact, it has been among the highly prejudiced that some of the most dramatic reversals of attitude have occurred.[14]

Proximity and Neighboring

Among the studies most frequently cited in support of the contact hypothesis are those studies of race and residence and, particularly, those studies of desegregated public housing. Many students of intergroup relations have argued that residential segregation occupies *the key* position in understanding the nature of contemporary race relations.[15] The Taeubers argue that residential segregation by color "not only inhibits the development of informal neighborly relations between whites and Negroes, but insures the (de facto) segregation of a variety of public and private facilities."[16]

The question of locating the ultimate determinant of racial status differentials is not at issue. The relevance of the urban segregation pattern to this study is its effect on the possibility that interracial equal-status contacts take place. The major assumption is that residential desegregation is an important and necessary prerequisite for the removal of barriers to effective communication and interaction between the races. Once these barriers are removed, a noticeable reduction of prejudice and a new gain in interpersonal relations should occur. However, it is primarily interpersonal contact (not residential environment per se) which is viewed as leading to a reduction of racial prejudice and stereotyped perceptions. If the races are kept separated, this "minimizes the number of situations in which whites are obliged to deal with Negroes, personally or symbolically, as equals or superiors."[17]

There have been essentially two types of research which have studied the effects of desegregated occupancy patterns and interracial neighborly contact: (1) studies of public housing residents and (2) studies of middle-income homeowners. The research of Deutsch and Collins first demonstrated the effects of residential desegregation in public housing, and their study remains the most widely cited in the literature.[18] The authors compared two desegregated low-rent projects in New York City with two biracial (internally segregated) projects in Newark, New Jersey. The focus of the Deutsch and Collins research was upon the differences in racial attitudes and their relationship to each type of occupancy pattern. Their results showed that residents in desegregated projects held more favorable attitudes toward members of the other race than did residents in the segregated projects. The overall outlook of the residents in the desegregated projects was more favorable on a number of counts: they displayed more friendly contacts between races, a greater willingness to engage in interracial associations, more favorability in their interracial attitudes, more tolerance toward living within a racially desegregated environment in general, and a closer sense of community within the projects.[19]

In a neighborhood or housing project where families live in close proximity, it is very difficult to disregard the characteristics and impressions of one's neighbors. This applies even in a highly heterogeneous neighborhood where one shares little in common with his neighbors and elects to minimize neighborly contact. Residential proximity has been shown to facilitate neighboring associations among families having homogeneous socioeconomic characteristics, even when residential mobility is high, as it often is in housing projects.[20] Whereas residential segregation prevents members of different races from becoming neighbors and from recognizing one another's symbolic equality, residential desegregation provides an environment where friendly interracial contacts are possible. Physical proximity, then, should be viewed as a catalyst; it requires of a majority of residents a reaction, favorable or unfavorable. Black and white residents may not respond favorably to desegregated living, but only when desegregation exists, can they have the opportunity to do so.

Just as residing in desegregated neighborhoods increases the awareness of members of the other race, it also increases the probability that some of these residents will engage in interracial neighboring. In a study similar to that of Deutsch and Collins, Wilner, Walkley, and Cook found that where equal-status neighborly contacts did occur between members of initially estranged groups, especially where there was a lack of opposition to such associations, interracial attitudes improved noticeably.[21]

Whereas the findings on the reactions of middle-class homeowners to residential desegregation are less relevant to our immediate interests, the findings of a number of these studies conducted in middle-income neighborhoods parallel those conducted within lower-income housing projects.[22] For example, a recent study by Meer and Freedman of a Stockton, California suburb reconfirms the contact hypothesis as it pertains to middle-income white homeowners. The authors found that when blacks and whites of equal socioeconomic status lived together in the same middle-income suburb, there was a marked tendency for the number of meaningful contacts between them to increase over time and for these contacts to lead to improved relations between the races.[23]

Previous Contacts

Whether or not individuals are willing to engage in informal relationships with members of another race is dependent upon more than the racial mix of the neighborhood in which they reside; it is also partly a function of their own past interracial experiences. Enduring residuals of individuals' past social experiences are frequently brought forth during critical periods of adjustment to new situations (entry into a desegregated neighborhood, for example). Sherif argues that it is a combination of past and present experiences that is responsible for an individual acquiring a perspective which enables him to operate within contemporary circumstances.[24]

Previous equal-status contact has been shown to be an important factor in explaining favorable racial attitudes in a variety of contexts, and a lack of such contact has been found useful in explaining a reluctance to engage members of the other race in relations which imply social equality. For example, in a study of a community in a southern state, a background lacking in equal-status contact was more related to negative racial attitudes than either low occupational prestige or low educational achievement.[25] Other studies — of white residents in a northern city, students in a large southern university, public housing residents, and white residents residing in neighborhoods adjoining the scene of a race riot — show that acceptance of, and favorable attitudes toward, black Americans are directly related to previous extended associations with members of that race.[26] Jahoda and West report that persons who had lived in close proximity to members of the other race prior to entering desegregated housing projects had far fewer expectations of racial hostility than those who were entering a "mixed" environment for the first time.[27]

Temporal Considerations

Attitudes and perceptions are not only the result of responses to a social-symbolic environment; they are also conditioned by the length of time persons remain therein. Other studies of desegregation in public housing have not reported the relationship between duration of residence and residents' racial outlooks. It seemed reasonable, in advance of the field work, to argue that the longer one resides in a desegregated housing project the greater will be the opportunity for this environment to affect his racial perspectives. Studies conducted in other neighborhoods show that duration of residence had an effect upon attitudinal and perceptual adjustment and the degree to which individuals, black and white alike, came to identify with their surroundings.[28]

There exists a second temporal consideration which is related to the attitudes of residents and can further qualify the effects contact has upon these attitudes. This is the consideration of whether residents arrive in a neighborhood prior to or after the process of desegregation begins. Hunt found that whites who moved into a northern suburb after black families had begun to enter showed "twice the proportion" of acceptance of integrated housing and far less resentment toward blacks than those white residents who lived there prior to the entrance of the first black families.[29] Fishman reports that in a New Jersey suburb perceived status fears and pressures from the "outside white world" caused many of the original white residents to leave after the community became increasingly desegregated.[30] Incoming black families in this same suburban neighborhood, however, reported status gains.[b]

Dimensions of Prejudice

Before we turn our attention to a brief discussion of reference groups and the

---

[b]Any analogy between middle-class suburbs and low-cost public housing cannot be carried too far. In contrast to the black families entering middle-income suburbs, none of the blacks entering public housing are buying their way out of segregated areas and into prestigous ones! In most cases, however, public housing apartments in Border City do provide better dwellings than are otherwise available to lower income black citizens. On the other hand, many low-income whites are likely to react similarly to the white suburbanites upon perceiving a threat to their limited status as a result of a "black invasion." For most Border City residents of both races, withdrawing from a desegregated project was not a readily available option, unless they were willing to accept substantially less in terms of housing.

role they play in the formulation and maintenance of individuals' racial outlooks, it is important to note that racial attitudes are multidimensional; peoples' tolerance or lack of tolerance differs depending upon the behavioral context in which interracial associations occur. In studies of the reactions of white middle-class residents to black families who were entering "their" neighborhood, researchers discovered that increased tolerance on the part of the newcomers' immediate neighbors did occur, but this attitude change was restricted to interracial *residential* attitudes per se and did not generalize to other dimensions of prejudice.[31] In other words, there was little evidence that blacks became more acceptable in more intimate behavioral contexts as an immediate result of interracial neighboring. The change of attitude with respect to having black neighbors tended not to spread from that one dimension to others, unless preceded by socially intimate contacts in those other areas. In their study, Meer and Freedman concluded that while white residents definitely developed a respect for blacks as neighbors, they tended to retain less tolerant attitudes with regard to other kinds of interracial contact.[32] For example, while residing next door to a black family of equivalent socioeconomic means came to be acceptable, engaging in more intimate social contacts, otherwise common to neighborhood couples, was rare. This failure for attitudes to readily generalize has been documented in a number of research settings,[33] and it is a consideration that we shall return to in our analysis.

Interracial Perceptions and "Significant Others"

The concept reference group enjoys considerable prominence in the social science literature. This is a concept that has been variously defined, but there is general agreement that a reference group is one to which an individual relates himself through affiliation and/or identification. In return, a reference group is said to serve him as a source of values which provides behavioral and attitudinal motivation and perspective in various social circumstances.[34]

Reference groups are, then, of importance to students of race relations. However, it is necessary to keep in mind that any given group is usually "segmentally rather than totally relevant to an individual's values."[35] Put in another way, different groups are used as reference groups in different social circumstances, and the guidelines they provide are often situation-specific. In a society that tends to be pluralistic, it is not likely that an individual will derive his motivations, perceptions, and appropriate behavior patterns from any single group. One group very rarely becomes a salient referent for all social behavior, except, perhaps, in the case of the extremist.[36]

A low-rent housing project becomes for its occupants a type of membership group; it may or may not become a significant referent with regard to one's personal perspective. In addition to other circumstantial factors, the probability that it will become such a referent is a function of the way residents relate to this membership group and to their other reference groups. For project housewives in Border City, especially those who hold no job, the project and its immediate neighborhood is the main social domain. Few women belong to outside groups; their most important reference groups tend to be kin and close friends.[c] Siegel and Siegel point out that, with the passage of time, attitudes tend to become more and more the product of membership group ("imposed group") influences.[37] This holds even in cases where the imposed group is not initially accepted. Consequently, despite the fact that other reference groups can insulate an individual from the effects of his immediate milieu, continued insulation can be maintained only if there is involvement and identification with these groups.

To the extent that a resident's housing project becomes a reference group,[d] it may be in conflict or accord with the way in which he perceives positions taken by his other reference groups. When a person's perceptions of his reference groups' positions are incongruent with the situation in which he finds himself, he may either withdraw from the situation or resort to rationalization. In cases where an individual comes to reside in desegregated surroundings for the first time, his gradual acceptance of the circumstances – his tolerance – may be the result of a felt need to rationalize and justify the situation.

Justification and rationalization serve pressing personal needs; they explain behavior and defend status. They amend perceived inconsistencies. To the degree that such a process of rationalization operates among project occupants, residents may react in one of two ways: they may interpret other reference groups as being tolerant of the racial environment in which they now live, or they may view those groups' opposing opinions as unimportant to their own views.[e] This strain toward consistency should be most apparent among residents who engage in interracial neighboring and whose "significant others" oppose such behavior.

---

[c]This fact is based upon the author's observations and subsequent data analysis.

[d]The issue of why it is that individuals adopt or fail to adopt certain of their reference groups' behavioral guidelines is also a concern in reference group research. See, for example, Robert K. Merton, *Social Theory and Social Structure*, Glencoe, Illinois: Free Press, 1957, p. 328.

[e]This is the type of resident reaction reported by Daniel M. Wilner, et al., "Residential Proximity and Intergroup Relations in Public Housing Projects," *Journal of Social Issues*, 8 (1952). Public housing tenants who were tolerant of racial desegregation either perceived others as having similar feelings or as being unimportant to the way they felt. Inconsistencies of perspective within the context of race relations are discussed in Isador Chein, et al., "Consistency and Inconsistency in Intergroup Relations," *Journal of Social Issues*, 5 (1949); a theory of perceived inconsistency and its resolution is presented in Leon Festinger, *A Theory of Cognitive Dissonance*, New York: Harper and Row, 1957.

Purpose and Hypotheses

The majority of studies investigating the reactions of residents to residential desegregation have viewed the feelings of middle-class white homeowners toward middle-class black families who have recently arrived in "their" neighborhoods. These studies have been conducted in neighborhoods where the process of desegregation has been, for the most part, gradual. Most conclusions concerning residential racial desegregation among lower income persons are based on several studies conducted in public housing projects nearly two decades ago.[38] In contrast to the aforementioned middle-class neighborhoods, desegregation in public housing has often been rapid, dramatic, and extensive.

The sites of the research reported here are municipal public housing projects in Border City, in which the desegregation process has recently been very rapid. The rapidity with which desegregation took place was primarily a consequence of the Civil Rights Acts of 1964 and the fact that sizeable numbers of black and white citizens were eligible to apply for low-rent public housing. As a result of federal legislation, occupants of low-rent public housing were to be assigned dwelling units according to need and without regard to race.[39] As a consequence of this imposed nationwide compliance, many towns and cities, having a biracial demand for low-rent housing and which were previously characterized by traditions of segregated public housing, began to experience desegregation within their municipal projects. Border City was one such city.

Racial prejudice and opinions concerning racial desegregation can largely be attributed to normative systems which differ from one sociocultural context to another and which alter their prescriptions with the passage of time. This suggests that at least two kinds of research regarding the interracial behavior and attitudes of public housing residents should be profitable: (1) replication of early studies conducted in northern states, now that we have experienced more than a decade of intense civil rights activities and racial unrest, and (2) studies conducted in other regions where racial desegregation of public housing has recently begun.

This monograph reports an attempt to partially fulfill the latter research need. Although it was not designed as a replication of any of the earlier public housing studies, its focus on interracial contact and its method permit comparison of findings.

Border City and its surrounding region are neither characterized by the traditional racial prejudices of the Deep South nor by the racial antagonisms that have recently emerged in the urban North. Thus the history and circumstances of this area of the country probably affect attitudes toward residential desegregation in a manner distinct from that of the southern or northern milieu.

In addition to examining the contact hypothesis in a new and different setting, the research attempted to overcome some of the shortcomings of previous studies which looked at this issue. Residential desegregation and interracial contact have been nearly exclusively viewed from the perspective of the white occupant. Despite the fact that there is some evidence to suggest that the similarities in the correlates of antiblack and antiwhite prejudice exceed the differences,[40] very few studies have examined black American or other minority group perspectives with regard to this issue of intergroup relations. This is certainly true of the analyses of residential desegregation. One of the few exceptions is the research of Works which dealt with black public housing occupants.[41] Even in the otherwise comprehensive study of Deutsch and Collins, only one-fifth of the respondents were black, and surprising little analysis is presented for them.[42]

From the outset, the design of the research reported here was to intentionally give equal attention to black and white responses to members of the other race and desegregated living; half the respondents are black and half are white. Both racial groups reside in public housing projects located in the same city. One of the primary foci of the research is the attitudes of black and white residents toward living with each other as neighbors. More than twenty years ago, Williams urged social scientists to study individuals' reactions to intergroup contacts which they were actually experiencing.[43] Too few researchers have followed this advice. Many studies have asked respondents to react to hypothetical situations involving contact with members of another race or ethnic group. In this study, the respondents were asked to react to a situation which was both real and visible. Residents were questioned about the residential desegregation that was, in fact, taking place in the neighborhood in which they were living. The respondents were adult women living in a housing community that was undergoing an extensive desegregation process.

A limitation in much of the intergroup relations research is the lack of comparability of minority group and dominant group respondents with respect to such variables as socioeconomic status and family structure. These racial differentials often make it difficult to interpret the meaning of attitude variations. White respondents, for example, have often been asked to record their attitudinal position toward blacks of equal social position — a category of people with whom they may be totally unfamiliar. The black and white residents studied here are generally comparable on "objective" measures of socioeconomic status, and it is to one another they are reacting. The screening of applicants for public housing assures a considerable degree of homogeneity among its residents.

The research for this book was guided by a considerable range of literature on intergroup antipathy and the effects of equal-status interpersonal relations between blacks and whites. In certain respects, this study is at once explanatory and exploratory. It is explanatory in that it empirically tests the generalization which has come to be called the contact hypothesis after first having specified this theoretical proposition within the research context and in terms of given variables. Our discussion has emphasized that certain meaningful and systematic relationships exist between certain behavioral-environmental variables and the subjective perceptions people have regarding interracial contact and residential desegregation. For analytical purposes, these variables are herein conceived as major determinants of persons' interracial attitudes and perceptions. The following general hypothesis was formulated in order to guide the field research and to specify relationships between measured variables in a readily testable form:

Tolerant attitudes by members of each race toward the other and the degree to which they perceive their reference groups as being tolerant of racial desegregation are positively associated with: (1) amount of interracial neighboring; (2) degree of previous equal-status contacts with members of the other race; (3) duration within a desegregated housing environment; and (4) an absence of perceived status threat from living in a desegregated residential surrounding.

This study may also be considered a case study of residential desegregation in a border state city. This is a topic that heretofore went unresearched for want of the opportunity; interracial contact has simply not been explored in this sociocultural environment. And, as will be argued, the findings of this research generate suggestions for reexamining some of our present generalizations concerning race relations.

2 The Border City Study

Border City

Border City is located within the most rapidly growing metropolitan county in the state; the current SMSA population exceeds 170,000 persons.[1] The county has had metropolitan status since 1950, and in the past twenty years has grown 75 percent larger — a growth rate more than twice that of the average rate of U.S. metropolitan counties. The city, located on a plateau west of the Appalachian foothills, serves as a service center for a number of small cities and towns which are tied to Border City by major highways.

As is true of many American cities, Border City's rapid growth has been correlative with and facilitated by outward expansion. The city contains a stable black population, which for the past thirty years has accounted for a fourth of the total inner-city population. Only one-in-ten black families reside outside of the central city limits. At the time the data were collected, no middle-income black families lived in outlying subdivisions, except for those living in the city's one small all black middle-class neighborhood.

Except in public housing projects and on a few lower-income blocks, blacks and whites lived on streets and in neighborhoods comprised entirely of members of their own racial group. There was no evidence to indicate that the comparative socioeconomic status of the races or the degree of residential segregation in Border City was significantly different from that generally found in the "average" American city. In their study of urban residential segregation, Taeuber and Taeuber[2] found that the 207 cities they examined ranged between a low of 60.4 and a high of 98.1 on their index of segregation (100 representing "perfect" segregation by block). The median index for these American cities was 87.8, nearly identical to the index for Border City.

The Public Housing Projects

Federally financed public housing in Border City was comprised of 1319 apartments located throughout seven projects. Each of the seven projects in the city was maintained and administered by a central housing authority. The racial composition of the projects is ultimately determined by the policy of assignment employed by the local housing authority. Prior to 1965, the resident assignment policy was one of maintaining racially segregated projects. In each of the years 1937, 1941, and 1954 two "sister" projects were completed — one for blacks

15

and the other for whites. A seventh project, opened in 1966, had no "racial tradition."

As a consequence of the Civil Rights Act of 1964, the established public housing segregation pattern was changed. However, the process of desegregation had not progressed uniformly throughout the projects. The three "black projects" remained completely segregated, while in the three "white projects," 234 of the 558 families had been "displaced" by blacks. Public housing in Border City had become predominantly black in little more than two years. The controversy attending this desegregation process is discussed in chapter 3, and consequences of this "black invasion" are considered at length in the concluding chapter.

Despite the rapid influx of black families into formally all white projects, the proportionate distribution of the races within individual projects reflected a variety of occupancy patterns. From the tenants' viewpoint, the population was readily divisible into six categories (table 2-1): segregated black (Washington Park); segregated white (Green Tree East); desegregated black and white (both residents of John Harrison); minority group black (Green Tree West); and minority group white (Washington Park Addition). ("Minority group" residents are those who represent a numerical minority in a project comprised of members of the other race.)

Table 2-1
Identification of Housing Projects, Number of Respondents, Sampling Ratios, and Completion Rates

Project Name[a]	Racial Composition	Number of Respondents	Sampling Ratio[b]	Completion Rate[c]
Washington Park	Segregated Black	33	.17	.75
Green Tree East	Segregated White	33	.51	.75
John Harrison	Desegregated Black	35	.19	.80
John Harrison	Desegregated White	34	.23	.77
Green Tree West	Minority Black	17	–	.89
Washington Park Addition	Minority White	16	–	.76

[a]The project names are pseudonyms.

[b]The ratio of the number of residents interviewed to the total number of residents in the population subgroup.

[c]The percentage of assigned interviews completed.

Table 2-1 shows the projects selected for study, the sampling ratios and the completion rates for each respondent category. Because John Harrison (a former mayor of Border City), the city's largest project, was the only one in which the racial ratio approached 0.50 (0.56 black/0.44 white), both the desegregated black and white samples were drawn from it. The Green Tree project was analytically divided into two sections, referred to as Green Tree East and Green

Tree West. At the time of the field work, there were no longer any projects that did not have black residents. Green Tree had a few black families; none were located in any particular buildings, although they all resided in a particular section of the project. An imaginary line was drawn dividing the project into two sections. As a result of interviewing in the segregated white section (Green Tree East), it became apparent that this analytical division was perceived by many of the tenants as real. Their definition of what constituted their project tended to exclude the western half of the project.

The municipal housing projects are not all contiguously located. Of the four projects from which the samples were drawn, two (Washington Park and Washington Park Addition) are located within Border City's largest black neighborhood. Whereas the other two (Green Tree and John Harrison) are located within a census tract that contains nearly equal numbers of blacks and whites, virtually all of whom live on segregated blocks. Aside from the differences in racial composition, these two areas are both inside the city limits, are older sections of the city, have comparatively high population densities and are very similar with regard to the socioeconomic characteristics of their residents. Life in each of the four projects is essentially similar. However, the projects do vary in some respects. A brief description of each project follows:

Washington Park contains 206 apartments in twenty-eight two story brick buildings with six or eight families in each building. The project was constructed in 1941 and is located in the aforementioned predominately black neighborhood. Characteristic of all projects, there are no center hallways; each apartment has its own outside entrance. Individual buildings are separated by concrete walks and drying areas for laundry. The project provides no machine washing or drying facilities. (This is true for all other projects, as well.) There is a small play area for children located in one of the center courts of the project. A branch office of the housing administration is located in one of the buildings which also houses the power plant and maintenance shop for the project. The resident manager and his secretarial and operations staff are black. Across a busy two-lane thoroughfare is a line of small stores and businesses, including a pharmacy, a grocery, a laundromat, a liquor store, and a barber shop.

Washington Park Addition is comprised of twenty-two brick buildings capable of housing 150 families. It was completed immediately prior to the study. It is located directly adjacent to Washington Park; its buildings are somewhat smaller in size and are separated by walks, several asphalt parking lots and a circular drive. The buildings contain six or eight apartments. The apartments on either end of the buildings are one-story and have one bedroom, whereas the middle units in each building have two stories and include two and three bedroom apartments. In one corner of the lot is a building containing eight efficiency apartments for elderly couples. The resident manager and staff are the same as those for Washington Park.

Green Tree is one of the two original projects built under the WPA in 1937. It is located across the city from Washington Park in a racially mixed neighborhood. It is comprised of twenty-five buildings with four to eight apartments. Most of the buildings are single story brick and face the street on either side of a paved road which encircles the project. Each apartment has its own fenced backyard with drying areas for laundry. In this respect, Green Tree provides its residents with a bit more privacy than other city projects. Bordering on the project to the north and east are single-family lower-class homes, to the south is the playground which serves the five projects in the immediate area, and to the west is located Green Tree's sister project — occupied entirely by blacks. The main office of the housing administration is located on the north end of the project. The director and her female staff are all white, and the maintenance staff has few black employees.

John Harrison, built in 1954, is the city's largest project. It contains 370 apartments in 53 two-story brick buildings, with four to ten families in each building. It is the only fully desegregated project and not only had nearly equal numbers of black and white occupants, but the races were desegregated from an ecological perspective as well. The occupancy pattern gave the impression that families of both races had been "randomly" distributed throughout. There were very few cases of buildings being occupied exclusively by whites or blacks. John Harrison is located in the same neighborhood as Green Tree, touches on the same playground, and is directly supervised by the same personnel. It has no resident manager of its own. Walks and drying areas separate the buildings. The coal-storage yard and central heating plant (for all projects located on this side of the city) are located immediately adjacent to this project. The apartment buildings were constructed on either side of two city streets which together form a large oval, approximately a quarter mile in length. The buildings are positioned face to back, with the end units facing the street.

Sampling and Interviewing in Public Housing

The population from which samples were drawn consisted of all housewives[a] who resided in public housing at the time of a preliminary survey especially designed for the study. The race of each household in the projects and the location of vacant apartments were designated by a team of "area workers" from the Border City Community Action Program three months before interviewing began. The public housing authority files were not made available to the researcher. The women interviewed included a small number of newcomers to the projects who arrived after the preliminary survey. However, there were few

---

[a]The author acknowledges the neglect of the black male in much of social science research and agrees fully with those who argue that it is necessary to examine his role firsthand in order to achieve a more thorough understanding of the black community and its subculture. The decision to interview housewives was largely determined by the fact that many project apartments were without adult males and/or children, but less than one percent were without housewives. In addition, it is these women who are chiefly responsible for initiating and reacting to contacts that arise from sharing the project with their neighbors.

instances of occupants who had been displaced by members of the other race. The term "housewife" is used to refer to a woman who principally attends to the domestic affairs of the home; this includes women with and without children, married and single, living with or without male partners.

A random sample of forty-four apartments was drawn from the resident categories designated segregated black, segregated white, desegregated black and desegregated white.[b] A sampling frame for each of these categories was constructed from project site plan projections provided by the City Planning Office. The apartment and building designations were placed on these projections, and a code was developed to indicate the race of each resident household and the vacant apartments.

The two remaining resident categories, the minority group black and minority group white, represented a small number of occupants in their respective projects. Site projections were used to locate these residents living in projects occupied predominantly by members of the other race. All the housewives in these two categories whom the interviewers were able to contact were interviewed. In much of the analysis, these minority group residents are included in the "desegregated" groups.

In addition to the recorded observations of the author and interviewers, the chief source of data was the interview schedule (see the Appendix). It was comprised primarily of "forced choice" items but included a number of open-ended questions which allowed respondents to evaluate issues in their own words. A number of these questions were principally included for developing a focused context of discussion. Several sets of questions were adopted from the instrument used by Deutsch and Collins and suitably modified for the present study.[3] During the two months before the interviewing began, the author spent several weeks talking to housing administration personnel, resident managers, maintenance staff, project adolescents, and selected residents.

The interview schedule took, on the average, between 45 minutes and one hour to administer, excluding the interviewer's introduction and whatever discussion ensued. Two young black women were employed to interview the black housewives and the author interviewed the white respondents.[4] Both women had college training and former experience interviewing in field situations. After the interviewing began, a comparison of notes with female interviewers uncovered no handicap due to the researcher's sex, except that entry into homes was gained with less initial suspicion by female interviewers. Two extensive interviewer training sessions were held prior to a pretest. The pretest schedules were administered in projects which were not to be sampled

---

[b]The decision to draw samples of this size was determined by a projected completion rate based upon the pretest and available funds. Whereas the resulting N's for the various subgroups are not large, the primary interest in this research was the comparison of data from analytical categories and not that of generalizing to the entire population of residents. Confidence in such comparative analysis is enhanced when there is relative homegenity among subgroups with respect to relevant control variables. Such homogeneity is demonstrated in chapter 3.

for the study. Whereas the quality of the pretest schedule was generally good, and the pretest provided a number of valuable insights, those data are not presented in the tabular analysis.

The 168 respondents were interviewed during a two-month period in late spring and early summer 1967. As shown in table 2-1, the completion rate for all respondent categories was at least 75 percent of the apartments selected. Before an apartment was excluded from an interviewer's list, at least three attempts were made to find the housewife at home: the initial call and two callbacks, each at different times of the day. Despite some early concern that the nature of the interviews might cause detrimental rumors to spread, no such obstacle arose.[c] Interviewers were generally viewed suspiciously upon their initial entry into each project,[d] but the ease of gaining access to respondents' homes increased after suspicions were allayed. The acceptance afforded all interviewers and the rapport maintained throughout the vast majority of the lengthy interviews was exceptionally good. No problems arose that were of serious proportion. The remainder of this chapter is devoted to a presentation of the measurement of the independent and dependent variables used to test the contact hypothesis.

Independent Variables

Interracial Neighboring

The amount and kind of neighboring in which housewives engaged was measured by responses to a series of interrelated questions (Appendix, items 35 and 38). Interviewers probed tactfully for interracial contacts and for the particular circumstances under which they occurred. Each woman living in a desegregated project received a score showing the extent of her interracial neighboring. Table 2-2 presents the scoring technique. A simple weighting method was employed to differentiate the degrees of social exchange implied in various kinds of neighborly behavior and the frequencies with which that behavior occurred. Each housewife was assigned a score ranging from 0 (no interracial neighboring) to 23 (many interracial neighboring contacts). Housewives who initiated

---

[c]Each interviewer carried a letter of introduction and identification certifying him as a field worker for a research project sponsored by the university located in Border City. The major reasons which prevented interviewers from completing their assigned interviewers were that prospective respondents were repeatedly not at home or they were ill or disabled.

[d]Public housing residents were beset regularly by teams of solicitors and just as regularly by bill collectors. The area's high delinquency and crime rates caused many housewives who were alone at home to be hesitant about allowing persons into their homes.

interracial neighborly visits received a somewhat higher score than if they only received a caller of the other race. The more regularly such contacts occurred, the higher the respondent's score.[e]

Table 2-2
Classificatory Index Used to Rate the Degree and Kind of Interracial Neighboring

Schedule Item					
Persons known best in project – who are members of other race	None (0)[a]	One acquaintance (1)	One friend or two acquaintances (3)	Two acquaintances and a friend (6)	All friends (8)
Persons known "pretty well" – members of other race	None (0)	One or two (1)	Three-four (2)	Five + (3)	
Housewife visits with member of other race	None (0)	Less than once a week (2)	Every couple days (3)	Every day or more (4)	
Member of other race visits with housewife	None (0)	Less than once a week (2)	Every couple days (2)	Every day or more (3)	
Housewife helps out member of other race	Never (0)	Yes (3)			
Member of other race helps out housewife	Never (0)	Yes (2)			

[a] Figure within parentheses = weighted score assigned housewife for the particular behavior.

Previous Equal-Status Contacts

The measure of previous interracial equal-status contacts was derived from a multipart question (Appendix, item 27) designed to provide an inventory of past experiences wherein the respondent related to members of the other race in a manner implying social equality. Respondents were specifically asked to recall whether or not they had had contacts with members of the other race in other neighborhoods, on jobs, while in school, as playmates during childhood, and as adult friends. Interviewers led into this series of probes by asking respondents if they could recall any interracial contacts they had had previous to moving to the project. Many respondents discussed one or more of their previous life experiences involving such contacts without additional questioning. In such cases, probes for particular areas were simply used as a checklist. When a

---

[e] Tabular analysis (chapter 4) was based upon a further reduction of respondents into one of three categories based on the total score: 1-3 points, "Few Contacts," 4-9 "Several Contacts," 10 or more points, "Many Contacts."

housewife reported having related to a member of the other race within one of the given areas, it became the interviewer's task to determine how well such a relationship met the criterion of "equal-status."[f] From an analysis of the responses, a simple classificatory index was contructed to differentiate housewives according to the intent of their previous interracial equal-status contacts. (table 2-3).[g]

Table 2-3
Classificatory Index Used to Rate the Kind and Degree of Previous Interracial Equal-Status Contact

Content	Score[a]
Never lived near a family of the other race	0
Lived in same neighborhood or same block	1
Lived across the street, next door or same building	2
Never worked on a job with a member of other race	0
Worked in same place, but no equal-status implied	1
Worked on job where equal-status clearly implied	2
Husband never worked on a job with member of other race	0
He worked same place, but no equal-status implied	1
He worked on job where equal-status clearly implied	2
Never had members of other race in school class	0
Did have members of other race in school class	1
Never had members of other race as playmates	0
Did have members of other race as playmates	1
Never had friends members of other race	0
Did have friends members of other race	1
Husband never had friends members of other race	0
Husband did have friends members of other race	1

[a]Maximum score possible varies from 7 for woman without husband present to 10 for woman living with husband.

---

[f]This flexibility given the interviewer is characteristic of the interview schedule, as contrasted with the questionnaire. The interviewer was encouraged to respond to respondents' cues throughout the interview.

[g]For the analysis using previous equal-status contacts, the following classification of housewives was used:

	Assigned Score	
Degree of Previous Equal-Status Contact	Husband Present	No Husband Present
"Little-None"	0 - 2	0 - 1
"Some"	3 - 5	2 - 4
"Considerable"	6 or more	5 or more

Duration of Residence

Determining what constituted a "long" duration within desegregated public housing was governed by two factors: the residential turnover rate and the fact that little desegregation had occurred until two years prior to the field work. Discussions with the housing director, staff, and residents, together with a preliminary examination of the data, suggested that an established or "long-time" resident could be considered one who had lived in the same project for more than a year. In the data analysis, the following duration categories were used: one year or more, seven months to a year, and six months or less.

Dependent Variables

Racial Prejudice

A set of four social distance scales was used to measure the racial prejudices of black and white respondents (table 2-4). The scale items were developed by Westie[h] and have subsequently been used in different research settings, with respondents varying from college students to black adults in a midwestern city.[5] The six items in each scale have the advantage of being applicable to both black and white respondents (by alternating the object of prejudice from "average white adult" to "average Negro adult"). Such substitution of one race for the other is made possible by the fact that items for these scales were selected on the basis of judgments of items rather than attitudinal responses to items; the selection and judgment was that used in the Thurstone technique. Unlike the Thurstone technique, each item, regardless of the social distance it is judged to reflect, is assigned equal weight.[6]

A five-alternate-response pattern was used for each scale. A score of 24 on a scale indicates maximum racial intolerance and a score of 0 indicates maximum racial tolerance. A composite racial prejudice score can readily be computed (having a range from 0 - 96, from least to most prejudice) or each scale can be analyzed according to the dimension of prejudice it measures.[7] The items given in table 2-4 in a descending order of tolerance were presented to the respondent in a random order.[i]

---

[h]Although the scale items were identical, their administration varied as is described. Retests on samples to which the scales were administered showed them to be consistently reliable.

[i]Early in the pretest, it became apparent that many housewives found it difficult or impossible to choose among alternate responses when presented a card on which they were printed. Consequently, interviewers were instructed to use their judgment in assigning a respondent to one of the five alternatives. In cases where it was not immediately apparent, probes were used to determine the intensity of a respondent's attitudinal position.

Table 2-4

Social Distance Scales Illustrating Cumulative Ordering of Items and Scoring

Items	Alternative Responses[a] and Their Scores				
"I would be willing to have the "average" (Negro) (white) adult	SA (0)	A (1)	U (2)	D (3)	SD (4)

Residential Scale

. . . . live in my apartment building.
. . . . .live across the street.
. . . . live in my neighborhood.
. . . . live in my end of town.
. . . . live in my town.
. . . . .live in my country.

Positional Scale

. . . . as President of the U.S.[b]
. . . . as Congressman from my district.
. . . . as councilman on my city's council.
. . . . . . as head of the local community chest drive.
.as a member of a Red Cross committee in my town.
. . . as a member of a national patriotic organization.

Physical Scale

. . . . .use the same towel that I use.
. . . . swim in the same pool as I do.
.have her hair set by the same person that does mine.
.try clothes on at the same store where I buy clothes.
. . . . ride in the same crowded elevator I am in.
. . . . use lending library books I also borrow.

Interpersonal Scale

. . . . .as a close personal friend.
. . . . .as a dinner guest in my home.
. . . . as a person I might often visit.
. . . . .as an acquaintance.
. . . . .as someone to say hello to.
. . . . as someone I might see on the street.

[a]Strongly Agree, Agree, Undecided, Disagree, Strongly Disagree.

[b]It was necessary to add the person in question also had the capability. This, of course, was perceived to be someone other than "average."

Perception of Reference Groups' Position on Residential Desegregation

In addition to administering the attitude scale, interviewers classified each respondent according to her perception of the position her reference groups held with regard to racially desegregated occupancy patterns (Appendix, item 30). She was asked to carefully consider five reference groups: immediate family, close friends, other relatives, neighbors, and work associates (if any).[j] The questions and related probes were designed to portray *perceptions* of respondents. It was their assessment of positions these groups took that was important, not whether or not their perceptions were accurate.[k]

Interviewers' judgments were relied upon as they were in assessing attitudinal position. The schedule items often served as a checklist which interviewers used in judging, from the context of the interview, the respondents' perceptions of their reference groups' positions.

Each respondent was assigned a summary score representing the perception of her reference groups' positions concerning residential desegregation. For most analyses the following categories were used: "Tolerant," "Mixed Feelings," and "Opposed." The reference groups were characterized as tolerant of or opposed to residential desegregation when the majority of a respondent's reference groups were judged as being on a given side with respect to this issue. Perceived reference group position was said to be mixed, or ambiguous, when fewer than three of the groups were judged as holding opinions clearly tolerant or the reverse, or when a respondent was unable to clearly perceive the direction of their positions.

---

[j]During the pretest and the actual survey, attempts were made to isolate other reference groups or individuals who occurred to a substantial number of respondents to be significant in this way; very few were mentioned as a result of such probes.

[k]A related research interest was determining the amount of influence these five groups had upon respondents' racial opinions (Appendix, item 31). As shown, an attempt was made to assess the degree of influence indirectly by asking whether or not they agreed with the groups' positions and whether or not they discussed the issue with members of those groups. This question of influence was not used in subsequent analysis because exceedingly few respondents (2 percent) disagreed with their reference groups' positions, and those who did not discuss the issue were few and randomly dispersed throughout the subgroups. The variable of perceived influence did not specify the relationships.

3 Housewives in Public Housing

Before presenting a test of the contact hypothesis (chapter 4), it remains to familiarize the reader with the respondents and with the context within which the research was conducted. This chapter is devoted to a brief description of the controversy surrounding Border City's public housing and its housing authority, the admissions criteria and regulations pertaining to tenants, a comparison of black and white resident families on certain selected socioeconomic and family variables, and residents' attitudes toward life in public housing.

A History of Controversy[a]

Unlike some of the very large high-rise municipal projects in such cities as Chicago, St. Louis, New York, and Newark, there was never any widespread public concern over public housing in Border City. In fact, located where they were, many middle-income residents did not realize that there were any low-rent housing projects in the city. However, for a minority of citizens, including local politicians, educators, planners, and members of such groups as the League of Women Voters and the Human Rights Commission, the administration of public housing and the welfare of the tenants had frequently been controversial issues over the thirty year period since the first projects were opened.

Border City was one of forty U.S. cities, preselected by the WPA (Works Progress Administration), in which one of the initial fifty-one federally financed public housing projects was built. From the outset, low-rent housing was a source of administrative, political, and financial contention. This is reflected in the fact that five of the six members of the City Housing Commission resigned in protest upon the appointment of a former Internal Revenue collector as project manager. Less than a month after the Green Tree project opened (1937), the city manager complained to the federal Public Housing Administration that rents needed to be raised if the municipality was to provide adequate police and fire protection, garbage collection, sewage disposal, and access to public schools for tenants' children.[b]

---

[a]Unless otherwise indicated, the sources of data presented here are one or a combination of the following: a newspaper clipping file on local public housing 1937-1967; selected minutes of the Border City Municipal Housing Commission; materials provided by the Border City Human Relations Commission; reports prepared by the League of Women Voters Committee on Community Planning; and interviews with the director of the local Public Housing Authority, several city commissioners and interested citizens, and the assistant Secretary of Intergroup Relations, U.S. Department of Housing and Urban Affairs.

[b]From the rents, all local housing authorities pay operating expenses. In addition, a payment is made to the municipal taxing body, in lieu of a property tax, to cover these municipal services.

Throughout its history the public housing program in the U.S. has been denounced by critics of different persuasions. One traditional criticism takes the view that public housing is nothing other than a costly subsidy to the poor ("undeserving" understood) and as such is bad economics. This was essentially the position espoused by an influential city commissioner and mayor of Border City who held office during the 1950s and 1960s. If one looks at the way in which municipal low-rent projects are financed and managed, the program more nearly resembles a business loan or subsidy than it does a family-oriented charity or welfare program.

The Housing Act of 1937 clearly placed the responsibility for the development, ownership, and management of low-rent housing on the municipality.[1] City housing authorities are considerably more autonomous with respect to their policies and procedures than many would suspect. The federal government may loan up to 90 percent of the total project development costs; when 90 percent completed and certified inspected, the local authority (with the advice of the Public Housing Administration) sells its bonds on the private market. From the money received, the authority repays the federal loan plus interest. The overriding concern of public housing administrators is managing the projects in such a way that costs (maintenance, repairs, clerical expenses), vacancies, and turnover rates are minimized. The implication of this emphasis upon cost reduction for tenants is discussed in the following section.

The controversy concerning the local public housing authority reached its peak in the winter of 1960-61 with a public probe of the administration. This resulted in five counts of falsifying reports to the USPHA being brought against the director and his subsequent resignation. He was accused of contracting for equipment with an in-law in exchange for a percentage of the sales. Shortly thereafter, several members of the Municipal Housing Commission resigned from that body in a protest which revolved about awarding the director terminal leave pay. Some months later, an individual who had worked with the Housing Authority since the projects opened, assumed the position of director. Although this appointment was held suspect by a number of critics of the local Housing Authority, relatively little controversy surfaced for several years concerning public housing. The passage of the Civil Rights Act of 1964 followed shortly by federal approval for the construction of another project were to change this.

A number of civil rights organizations together with the Human Rights Commission and the League of Women Voters intensified their efforts in behalf of racial open occupancy subsequent to the 1964 Act. Whereas a major concern of these groups was identifying restrictions that operated in order to prevent working-class and middle-income black families from entering segregated white residential areas, they were also interested in the racial occupancy patterns and policies in public housing. This interest arose quite naturally due to the official policy of segregating projects by race which had only recently been officially abandoned and also to the fact that Washington Park Addition was soon to be completed in the predominantly black neighborhood. These proponents of open occupancy came to look at the way these new apartments would be assigned as a test case. At the time the research reported here began, the local Housing Authority director and a number of the staff felt unduly harassed by these civil rights organizations. The civil rights groups, on the other hand, were highly suspect that the authority's reluctance to cooperate with any study of open occupancy probably indicated its opposition to desegregation within the projects.

First Come – First Served and Desegregation

At the insistence of the federal government, local housing authorities were required to adopt tenant selection plans that were nondiscriminatory. Partly as a result of local pressures from Border City's chapter of CORE (Congress on Racial Equality) and the Human Rights Commission, the Housing Authority adopted a "first come – first served" plan: (1) all applications were filed by apartment size (position of an application was determined by rules for determining priority presented below); (2) the first applicant in each list received the first available apartment of that size; (3) applicants were not asked nor allowed to indicate preferences beyond size; and (4) applicants could refuse the first apartment available and retain their first priority, but they had to accept the second apartment offered or be moved to the bottom of the list. This plan was approved by the federal government as one that indicated movement toward an "integrated policy."

The trend toward increasingly black-occupied projects, discussed in chapter 2, continued after the adoption of the first come – first served policy. It was somewhat difficult to determine whether this trend was due entirely to the fact that fewer whites than blacks applied for apartments and fewer blacks moved out (as the Housing Authority insisted) or due to the fact that the fourth clause in the first come – first served policy was not being adhered to (as some critics suggested). Nonetheless, there was evidence to suggest that the authority's position provided a feasible explanation. Border City was in the process of implementing stricter code enforcements in order to obtain federal funding for urban renewal. Because nearly 20 percent of the city's housing units were rated as substandard and a large proportion of these families which were displaced or about to be displaced were black, this would substantially increase the number of eligible black families on the waiting lists. This trend is not unique to a few cities with public housing, but it appears to be a nationwide phenomenon. At its inception, public housing was not exclusively defined as black or minority group housing due to the fact that so many poor were working-class whites thrown out of work by the Depression. However, in 1970, black and other minority families accounted for more than 60 percent of public housing residents.[2]

That black families tend to remain in public housing longer is suggested by the fact that we interviewed a number of second generation and two third-generation black project dwellers. No second or third generation white residents were interviewed. If there was a larger number of black applicants and if their numbers were growing due to urban code enforcement and renewal dislocations, then once the policy of maintaining segregated projects was abandoned, one could expect the black/white ratio to increase. "Open occupancy" in middle-income white areas means something quite different from that of low-income public housing projects. A "racial balance" (something approximating 50/50 black white) could not be expected to be attained by following a first come — first served policy.

To Enter and Remain

In addition to requiring that applicants be city residents for a minimum of six months, applicants had to document the fact that their total household income was no more than the established limits (table 3-1). Those seeking access to the projects had to demonstrate that they were either without a dwelling place or resided in one judged inadequate by the Housing Authority.[c] Among those applicants meeting these requirements, priority was given within each apartment size category to persons displaced from former homes by local or federal government action and then to war veterans, servicemen, or their widows.

Table 3-1
Maximum Annual Household Income Limits for Admission and Continued Occupancy in Public Housing According to Family Size[a]

Number of Persons to Occupy the Apartment	For Admission	For Continued Occupancy
1	$3000	$3750
2	3900	4875
3	4200	5250
4	4400	5500
5	4600	5750
6	4800	6000
7	4900	6125
8	5000	6250
9	5100	6375
10 or more	5200	6500

[a]These figures are less child care exemptions, which allowed heads of households to deduct from their reported monthly income $10 for one minor dependent, $15 for two, $20 for three and $25 for four or more dependent children.

Whereas public housing families were hardly economically "well off," neither

---

[c]Inadequate was generally taken to mean dilapidated or deteoriating by Bureau of the Census standards. It also was determined, to a degree, by a consideration of overcrowding. The information concerning entrance and residency requirements was provided from literature given potential applicants and from the director of the Housing Authority.

could they be considered destitute. All households were required to pay one month's rent plus a minimum deposit of five dollars before moving into their assigned apartments. Table 3-1 gives the maximum household income limits for admission and continued occupancy.[d] A family was allowed to remain in public housing after its income exceeded the limit for admission but not after it went beyond the continued occcupancy limit. Further, once family income exceeded the annual limit for admission, rents were increased on a prorated basis, according to income increment and household size. At the time the data were collected, the minimum rent was 30 dollars and the maximum was 140 dollars. The average project household paid 60 dollars a month rent (including utilities). This is generally comparable to, although slightly higher than, the figures for all U.S. public housing projects.[3]

Whereas it might be exaggerating to argue that the Border City Public Housing Authority "creamed" the poor,[4] they did not house the city's poorest families. This is suggested by the stated income limits and was assured by the stability and perseverance most households had to maintain while waiting for an apartment and by the screening standards employed by the Housing Authority. Individuals were informed of the income limits and the necessity of providing proof of household income upon applying and periodically after entering the projects. At this time they were also familiarized with the tenant rules and responsibilities.[e]

Despite the fact that the tenant turnover rate was approximately 2.5 percent per month, the selectiveness of the screening process resulted in a tenant population which was not characterized by abject poverty but by households headed by regularly or fairly regularly employed persons whose income was insufficient to pay for adequate private housing. The major exceptions to this were a minority of households headed by the retired or the unemployable (handicapped), and those black households which could have afforded decent private housing but were shut out by residential segregation. Given the Housing Authority's emphasis upon cost efficiency, the larger the contingent of "stable, well-behaved" tenants the better. Of course, beyond this, the "ideal" household was the one where the breadwinner(s) earns more than the income limit for admission and not quite enough to have to leave the projects. A number of respondents alleged that the Housing Authority had its "favorites" whom it

---

[d]This schedule closely approximates the federal guidelines which suggest that household income not exceed five times the rent paid at admission except in cases where there are three or more dependents. These admissions rates were approximately $200-400 lower than rates for Chicago and New York projects.

[e]These tenant regulations and responsibilities were specifically spelled out in a brochure issued to all incoming tenants and they included: items tenants were responsible for replacing or repairing at their expense (light bulbs, window glass, window and door screens); maintenance tenants were obliged to do or pay extra for having done (mowing and trimming yard; if applicable, washing windows, cleaning and defrosting refrigerators); a list of prohibitions (no firearms, no pets, no interior decorating, no overnight guests, no loud radio, TV, etc.); and a series of general recommendations on how to be a thoughtful and responsible tenant.

permitted to stay on after their income exceeded the continued occupancy limit. Whereas we have no evidence to indicate this ever took place, it does, among other things, indicate that some tenants were well aware of the "cost efficiency" policy of the management.

What are the primary reasons families leave their former dwellings and enter public housing? Table 3-2 gives the housewives' responses. Generally, black and white housewives offer similar reasons; sizeable numbers of both groups entered the projects either because their former home was condemned or classified as unfit or because they could no longer afford their rent or payments. As shown, many black housewives' responses indicated that they entered public housing primarily to get a place of their own because of the inconvenience of living under former arrangements. This usually meant that these tenants left because of overcrowding and insufficient facilities and/or she and her family did not "get along" very well within their previous household. On the other hand, a nearly equal number of white respondents said they were obliged to move for lack of

Table 3-2
Reason Housewife Left Her Last Dwelling and Moved to Public Housing

	Reason	Project and Race[a]			
		Segregated Black (percent)	Desegrated Black (percent)	Segregated White (percent)	Desegrated White (percent)
(1.)	Dwelling became unfit, was condemned	33	42	25	30
(2.)	Could no longer afford the rent or payments	12	13	18	12
(3.)	Considerable loss of income due specifically to illness or death of provider	3	2	45	34
(4.)	She and/or family wanted a "place of her own" – previously living with others and inconvenient	40	35	6	12
(5.)	Disability and/or old age necessitated more suitable dwelling	3	4	6	12
(6.)	No response	9	4	0	0
		100 (N = 33)	100 (N = 52)	100 (N = 33)	100 (N = 50)

[a]N's for desegregated Black and white projects include those women who were minority group residents within their projects, as well as those housewives who live in the fully desegregated project.

alternatives upon loss of income due to the death or extended illness of the breadwinner — a fact partially explained by the larger number of older white residents. These then were the "downwardly mobile" households. Those responses categorized under reason number 5 (table 3-2) indicate households wherein disabilities and/or old age were added to poverty.

A Comparison of Black and White Public Housing Tenants

This section presents a brief description of selected socioeconomic characteristics of the respondents and their families by race. We have already seen that public housing residents share certain similarities by virtue of the fact that they have gone through the admissions procedures. Nearly all of the housewives and their families also shared another common experience in that their "home town"[f] communities were in the border state in which Border City was located. More than half of the respondents were raised in Border City or one of the contiguous counties. However, many more blacks (59 percent) than whites (26 percent) were raised in the city. None of the blacks were raised in the rural Appalachian counties of the state whereas nearly a fifth of the white housewives were.

Table 3-3 shows that the majority of respondents were between the ages of 25 and 49 years. However, it is also clear from an examination of that table that there were more younger black respondents than there were white and more older white respondents than there were black. In fact, the median age of black housewives was between 30 and 31, whereas the median age of whites was between 40 and 41.[g] Twenty-six percent of the black housewives were 24 years old or younger, whereas only 4 percent of the white respondents were that young. In contrast, 10 percent of the black respondents were 60 years or older and 28 percent of their white counterparts were that old.

Half the respondents were married at the time of the study — 52 percent of the blacks and 48 percent of the whites (table 3-4). Twenty-five percent of the black respondents were either divorced or separated. Twenty-three percent of the whites reported separations and divorces. Approximately three times as many blacks reported being separated as divorced; nearly equal numbers of

---

[f]"Home town" refers to the community in which the respondent "grew up", i.e., spent most time while in school and/or before becoming an adult. The majority were born and grew up in the same community.

[g]There were a fairly large number of older women, many of whom were living alone, in Green Tree East. Their opinions and attitudes, however, did not differ significantly from those of other women in the same segregated project. They did partially explain black-white differentials regarding marital status, children in the household, and employment. At the time of the interviewing, a high-rise apartment for the older eligible public housing residents was being completed. Prior to this, apparently some attempt was made to set aside a group of smaller apartments for the older couples and single person households.

Table 3-3
Distribution of Black and White Housewives by Age

| | Black | | White | |
	Number	Percentage	Number	Percentage
19 years or younger	5	6	1	1
22-24 years	17	20	2	3
25-29 years	19	22	9	11
30-39 years	22	26	27	33
40-49 years	12	14	12	14
50-59 years	2	2	8	10
60 years or older	8	10	24	28
	85	100	83	100

whites reported separations and divorces. Whereas the so-called matrifocal family structure was a prevalent one in Border City public housing, it was no more characteristic of black households than of white. Many more white housewives were widowed than were black housewives. This is in accord with what one might expect considering the larger number of older white respondents.

Table 3-4
Distribution of Black and White Housewives by Marital Status

| | Black | | White | |
	Number	Percentage	Number	Percentage
Married	44	52	40	48
Separated	16	19	10	12
Divorced	5	6	9	11
Widowed	8	9	22	27
Single	12	14	2	2
	85	100	83	100

Table 3-5 pertains to the occupational status of the respondents' household. Section A and B refer to housewives and show that a majority of both black and white women held no jobs. Of those women who were employed, 33 percent of the blacks and 19 percent of the whites held full-time jobs; more than twice as many white housewives reported having regular part-time jobs or doing occasional work (18 percent) as did their black counterparts (8 percent). More women held service jobs than any other type of work. Fifty-one percent of the employed blacks were service workers and 39 percent of the whites. Whereas 39 percent of the whites were working in clerical or sales positions, only 9 percent of the black women held those kinds of jobs. Twice as many blacks as whites did household work or held operative positions.[h]

Table 3-5
Occupational Status of Black and White Households

A. Distribution of Black and White Housewives by Employment Status

	Black		White	
	Number	Percentage	Number	Percentage
Unemployed	50	59	52	63
Full time	28	33	16	19
Part time	6	7	10	12
Occasional	1	1	5	6
	85	100	83	100

B. Distribution of Employed Black and White Housewives by Occupational Categories

	Black		White	
	Number	Percentage	Number	Percentage
Clerical or sales	3	9	12	39
Service work	18	51	12	39
Household work	7	20	5	16
Operative	7	20	2	6
	35	100	31	100

C. Distribution of Black and White Housewives by Husband's Occupational Category

	Black		White	
	Number	Percentage	Number	Percentage
Service work	18	42	6	16
Laborer	5	12	6	16
Craftsman	7	16	8	22
Operative	7	16	0	0
Clerical	0	0	4	10
Retired	4	9	10	26
Unemployed	2	5	4	10
	43	100	38	100

A majority of husbands in the households of the respondents' worked as service workers, laborers, or craftsmen (table 3-5, C). Nearly equal proportions of black and white husbands worked as laborers and craftsmen, but many more blacks (42 percent) than whites (16 percent) were service workers. Whereas

[h]The occupational classifications are those of the U.S. Bureau of the Census. Most female "operatives" were pressers in dry cleaning stores.

relatively few white husbands held clerical jobs (10 percent), none of these type jobs were held by black men. More than twice as many whites were retired or otherwise unemployed; again, this is a function of the age differential between the groups.

It is clear from an examination of table 3-6 that black housewives and their husbands had considerably more formal schooling than their white counterparts. Two-thirds of the black housewives completed 11 years of school, and 48 percent graduated from high school. On the other hand, 56 percent of the white housewives received no more than an eighth grade education, and over a third received six or fewer years of formal education. The data on respondents' husbands show much the same pattern — black husbands had received considerably more years of schooling than their white counterparts. This disparity between the races, in terms of years of school attendance, is a partial product of the younger age and more urban background of blacks and also an indication of the difficulties that fairly well educated blacks have of locating decent low-income private housing in Border City.

Table 3-6
Years of School Attendance of Black and White Adults

A. Distribution of Black and White Housewives by Years of School Attendance

	Black		White	
	Number	Percentage	Number	Percentage
6 years or less	5	6	30	36
7 or 8 years	9	11	17	20
9 or 10 years	12	15	19	23
11 years	16	20	8	10
12 years or more	39	48	9	11
	81	100	83	100

B. Distribution of Black and White Housewives by Number of Years Husband Attended School

	Black		White	
	Number	Percentage	Number	Percentage
6 years or less	5	13	11	28
7 or 8 years	5	13	13	33
9 or 10 years	3	8	8	21
11 years	8	21	1	3
12 years or more	17	45	6	15
	38	100	39	100

Table 3-7 (sections A-C) shows the fertility of the respondents and the number of children in their households. There was little difference between the races with respect to fertility. Black mothers tended to have had fewer children, but they had more fertile years remaining than white respondents. And, again, their urban background may have explained some of this variation. As a group, black housewives had more preschool children and tended to have more school-age children living with them than did white housewives.

The admissions and screening procedures used by the Border City Public Housing Authority assure that tenant families have basically similar socio-economic characteristics regardless of race. The greatest disparity between black and white residents was with respect to age and education. Black housewives and their husbands were comparatively younger and had completed more years of schooling than their white counterparts. Thus black respondents had higher status than whites on this one "objective" measure of education. With few exceptions, housewives of both races were born and raised in the same border state. There was little difference in family size or structure by race. Black working women were more often employed on a full-time basis and in lower status jobs than were white housewives. This same status discrepancy tended to characterize their husband's jobs, but to a lesser degree than for women. In summary, the evidence shows that blacks and whites within the housing projects studied were essentially similar in terms of their socioeconomic status.

Housewives View Project Life

The average member of the reading and viewing public has an image of low-rent urban projects which is derived from recent disclosures of the sordid conditions which exist in several of the nation's largest high-rise developments. The struggle for personal dignity, the defeat, the danger and the isolation in their extremes which characterize the tenants' lives in these projects has been well-portrayed recently by Moore and by Rainwater.[5] Life in the Border City projects was, in comparison to these elevated, high-density nightmares, far more "normal," but, in comparison to other low-income and working-class neighborhoods in the city, life was disproportionately characterized by frustration, suspicion, fear, tension, and indignity. The level of tenant dissatisfaction ran high in the projects, and virtually every resident moved there as a "last resort." The remaining text and accompanying tables present a brief description of some selected attitudes and opinions housewives held regarding life in the projects.

Table 3-8 shows the way in which housewives compared the apartment in which they were living to their last place of residence outside the projects.[i] It is clear that a majority felt that the project apartments provided better comfort and facilities. Nonetheless, it is surprising that such a substantial minority

---

[i]A number of respondents had moved to their apartments from other apartments within the housing projects.

Table 3-7

Fertility of Housewives and Numbers of Preschool and School-age Children in Apartments by Race

A. Distribution of Black and White Housewives by Number of Children

	Black		White	
	Number	Percentage	Number	Percentage
None	4	5	6	7
One	17	20	11	13
Two	21	26	20	24
Three	17	20	15	18
Four	9	11	14	17
Five	5	6	6	8
Six or more	10	12	11	13
	83	100	83	100

B. Distribution of Black and White Housewives by Number of Preschool Children in Apartment[a]

	Black		White	
	Number	Percentage	Number	Percentage
None[b]	29	34	58	70
One	29	34	18	22
Two	15	18	5	6
Three	11	13	1	1
Four or more	1	1	1	1
	85	100	83	100

C. Distribution of Black and White Housewives by Number of School-Age Children in Apartment

	Black		White	
	Number	Percentage	Number	Percentage
None[b]	37	44	39	47
One	14	16	14	17
Two	15	18	19	23
Three	11	13	9	11
Four or more	8	9	2	2
	85	100	83	100

[a]Children under six years of age.

[b]Includes women without children and women whose children are older.

reported either no difference between their current project home and their former dwelling or that the project apartment was worse. Two reasons help explain this finding. First, quite a number of respondents in these two categories represented those households which we have described as downwardly mobile. Second, a number of respondents had difficulty divorcing their feelings for life in the project from their assessment of their apartments per se. A third factor may be relevant; that is, residents are not representative of the extremely poor.

Table 3-8
How Housewife Compares Her Project Apartment to Her Last Dwelling

Project Apartment is . . . . . in comparison	Project and Race			
	Segregated Black (percentage)	Desegregated[a] Black (percentage)	Segregated White (percentage)	Desegregated[a] White (percentage)
Better	52	65	64	66
About the same	18	25	15	22
Worse	24	10	21	12
No opinion	6	0	0	0
	100	100	100	100
	(N = 33)	(N = 52)	(N = 33)	(N = 50)

[a]In this table and the remaining tables in chapter 3, the N's for desegregated projects include those women who were minority group residents within their projects, as well as those housewives who lived in the fully desegregated project.

Respondents were asked to indicate the one aspect of project life they disliked the most. From an examination of table 3-9, a felt lack of privacy and excessive noise were the chief complaints of many residents of both races. If we combine the responses in this category with those pertaining to the physical inadequacy of the apartment unit, then from no less than one-fourth to nearly one-half of the respondents are most disturbed by life in their apartments. As has been shown in other research, many public housing housewives lead very circumscribed daily lives so that disturbances while in their apartment (noise, solicitors, inspections) and dissatisfaction with the apartment itself lead the list of grievances. No less so in the Border City projects. Under the circumstances, it might appear surprising that so many residents reported that nothing disturbed them in the projects. However, throughout the research it was found that many housewives were understandably reluctant to report anything that could be interpreted as critical of the Housing Authority. Those who had recently entered and those who had resided in the projects for a long time were usually most reluctant to criticize. However, other responses and comments made by these same respondents detracted from their "unqualified" satisfaction.

All or nearly all of the points of dissatisfaction were shared by most project dwellers. Table 3-9 presents the *most* dissatisfying aspect of project life. Next to discontent directly related to the apartments, a substantial minority of

Table 3-9
The One Aspect of Project Life the Housewife Dislikes Most

That one aspect is . . .	Project and Race			
	Segregated Black (percentage)	Desegregated Black (percentage)	Segregated White (percentage)	Desegregated White (percentage)
Lack of privacy and/or excessive noise	37	33	18	32
Delinquent and criminal behavior	6	9	15	20
Rent scale, excessive surveillance, or other administrative acts	12	17	0	10
Living with or fear of having to live with members of other race	0	6	27	14
Physical inadequacy of the apartment itself	9	2	6	6
Too distant from downtown	3	4	0	4
Nothing disturbing about project	27	29	34	14
No response	6	0	0	0
	100	100	100	100
	(N = 33)	(N = 52)	(N = 33)	(N = 50)

respondents mentioned either certain behavior of the Housing Authority or the extensive delinquency and crime in and around the projects. Racial desegregation or impending desegregation is of little or no major concern to black housewives whereas a sizeable minority mention this among whites. Interestingly, twice the proportion of whites in the segregated project (27 percent) as in the desegregated project (14 percent) cite desegregation as that thing they dislike most. Table 3-10 reports the change housewives would most like to see made in the projects, and the responses suggest the same areas of dissatisfaction.

Table 3-10 shows that a number of residents felt that the authority's regulations were too strict and that they should be entitled to greater latitude with respect to having overnight guests, social gatherings, etc. This source of discontent was widely shared if not listed as first priority for change. In this respect, tenants in the projects were denied the full round of privileges that most had come to associate with a home, even if that home were in a slum neighborhood. Many housewives perceived and others argued that there were more social amenities available to them in their former slum dwellings than in the projects. "Families" were "defined" in such a way for example, that two older women living alone who were good friends or kin, could not live in the same apartment.

The crime rates and especially juvenile crime rates ran high in the two

Table 3-10

The One Change the Housewife Would Like Most to See Made in Her Project

She would like to see . . .	Project and Race			
	Segregated Black (percentage)	Desegregated Black (percentage)	Segregated White (percentage)	Desegregated White (percentage)
Her apartment altered to make it quieter or more comfortable	43	29	22	26
More latitude granted residents by the administration (e.g., permit her house guests without asking permission)	18	15	15	4
The rent scale changed	12	8	3	6
Prohibit desegregation	0	0	24	20
Establish protection from juvenile crime	0	4	9	10
Provide more "conveniences" (e.g., washers and dryers)	0	2	0	14
"Undesirables" prohibited from living in her project	9	0	3	10
Nothing changed, everything as good as can be expected	18	34	24	10
No response	0	8	0	0
	100 (N = 33)	100 (N = 52)	100 (N = 33)	100 (N = 50)

neighborhoods in which the projects were located. Shops, automobiles, and project apartments and facilities were often the targets of delinquents. The rates of armed robbery and assault were also among the highest in Border City in the project neighborhoods. Project residents, especially women and the elderly had repeatedly requested through the Authority additional police protection for the after dark hours. The high incidence of vandalism coupled with the tenant fining procedures employed by the authority served to exacerbate resentment among tenants. For example, tenants were held responsible for broken window glass, screens, and outside lights as well as any damages to garden equipment "signed out" from the Housing Authority. Ultimately, it became a tenant's responsibility to identify the person responsible for such damages or pay for their repair.

Table 3-10 serves to reemphasize the significance the apartment had for many women.[j] A majority of the time spent at home — and for housewives without

---

[j]The vast majority of apartments the interviewers visited were very different from the stereotype lower-income household. They were generally tidy and very rarely messy or dirty, and more than a few could have been legitimately considered immaculate. The orderliness, of course, usually varied indirectly to the number of small children in the household. Most women not only spent an inordiante amount of time in the home, they apparently took pride in their role as homemakers.

jobs, this was virtually all of the time – was spent within or directly around the housewives' apartments. This was true due to the necessity of caring for children, fear of venturing far from home, a lack of alternatives or a combination of these factors. Consequently, acquaintances and "friendships" established in the projects were almost always determined by propinquity and the shared perspective of being a "project wife." Whereas, when asked whether they had more friends inside the projects or outside in Border City a majority of women answered "outside," most rarely visited with these individuals. In fact, the respondents' participation in the community at large was virtually nil. Exceedingly few belonged to any clubs or voluntary organizations and scarcely more attended church, even if they had done so regularly prior to entering the projects. This comparative "seclusion", especially for the unemployed, was the reason many housewives gave interviewers for their willingness to be interviewed at length.

Table 3-11 presents the respondents' reported feeling toward remaining in or moving from the housing projects. A substantial number of respondents elected each of the four alternative responses. Many of those housewives who claimed they would be satisfied to remain in the projects represented those households which expressed hope that project life would change for the better. They frequently meant by this that more of the "undesirable" families would move or would be asked to move by the authority. These women's fears and frustrations were linked to a segment of the project residents. These families display similar lifestyles and attitudes to those Moore calls the "respectables,"[6] and they are, not unexpectedly, those the Authority points out to others as "models." The group of housewives that claims to be dissatisfied and currently looking for another dwelling is generally comprised of those who are either negotiating with relatives or friends for another home, often times with the hopes or promise of a better paying job, or those who have been given eviction notices or warnings. The remaining two responses reflect the position of two groups of respondents and their families both of whom see few if any alternatives to living in public housing. On the one hand, there are those who have resigned themselves to remain; among these women are the young who are most depressed, desperate, and confused, and the elderly – with or without disabilities – who have few if any relatives and no place else to go. On the other hand, there are those women whose position is still one of the hope that they will be afforded the opportunity to leave the projects for something better in the future.

Table 3-12 characterizes the unsolicited comments on race and desegregation made by housewives to interviewers. Black housewives living in the segregated project were not prone to comment on white project dwellers in either a negative or neutral manner. Twenty percent of the black respondents in the desegregated project mentioned white residents, but without bitterness or resentment; only five percent made negative comments to the black interviewers. The interesting comparison is that between the white housewives living in the segregated project and those in the desegregated project. Is is among the former housewives that twice the proportion of unsolicited negative comments were

Table 3-11
The Housewife's Attitude Toward Remaining in or Moving from Her Project

	Project and Race			
She is . . .	Segregated Black (percentage)	Desegregated Black (percentage)	Segregated White (percentage)	Desegregated White (percentage)
Satisfied and hopes to remain	31	46	49	20
Dissatisfied and is looking for another place now	24	6	9	12
Resigned to remain due to lack of alternatives	15	19	15	22
Aspiring to move in the future but not very soon	27	29	27	46
No response	3	0	0	0
	100 (N = 33)	100 (N = 52)	100 (N = 33)	100 (N = 50)

made — paralleling the finding in table 3-9. It would appear that the threat of desegregation in public housing kindled more racial antipathy than its actual consequences.[k]

Table 3-12
The Housewife's Unsolicited Comments About Desegregation and Members of the Other Race[a]

	Project and Race			
She made . . .	Segregated Black (percentage)	Desegregated Black (percentage)	Segregated White (percentage)	Desegregated White (percentage)
No unsolicited comments	94	75	37	48
Especially bitter-negative comments	0	0	15	8
Negative comments	0	5	39	22
Reference to other race but without bitterness or resentment	6	20	9	22
	100 (N = 33)	100 (N = 52)	100 (N = 33)	100 (N = 50)

[a]Unsolicited comments refer to comments made by respondents early in the interview and prior to any mention of desegregation and members of the other race by the interviewer.

---

[k]The alternative explanation — whites in the desegregated project initially held more tolerant attitudes — is entertained in chapter 4.

This chapter provides a description of the context within which housewives in public housing lived their daily lives. It shows how the Authority's screening procedures provide a certain degree of tenant homogeneity, regardless of race, and how the rules and regulations help create project life styles for the "not-so-poor" which tend to be typified by solicitude, withdrawal, and indignity. We might think of the degree of regimentation and surveillance to which project dwellers are exposed as falling somewhere between that within a "total institution" and that a citizen experiences in the community at large. This contexual understanding is necessary in order to more adequately explain the nature and consequences of interracial contact within Border City municipal housing. In the next chapter, data are presented which test the contact hypothesis under the circumstances described above.

4

Contact, Prejudice, and Perceptions of Desegregation

This chapter reports the research findings based upon the interview data gathered from the 168 housewives in the public housing projects: 33 black and 33 white respondents living in racially segregated projects; 35 black and 34 white respondents living in the desegregated project; and 17 black and 16 white respondents residing in projects wherein they were the racial minority. More specifically, the contact hypothesis is tested by examining the effects that interracial neighboring, previous equal-status contacts, and duration of project residence have upon racial prejudice and opinions concerning residential desegregation. The reader may wish to refer again to the sections of chapter 2 which present the measures used for the major variables discussed in the analysis that follows. Throughout the chapter, the data are presented which test the general research hypothesis and its corollaries without extensive comment. Discussion and interpretation of the findings are reserved for chapters 5 and 6.

Interracial Neighboring

The major independent variable in the public housing study was the amount of interracial neighboring in which respondents engaged. In this section, its relationship to racial prejudice and to perceptions regarding residential de-segregation are examined. Interracial neighboring was defined as informal conversation, visits, and mutual assistance between black and white housewives. Within the context of the Border City projects, outlined in the preceding chapter, neighboring relationships must be understood as something less than interpersonal exchanges characterized by profound warmth, trust, and intimacy. The majority of neighboring contacts within the projects were those we would characterize as "passing-the-time-of-day" rather than close friendship relations, for, as we have seen, there was a decided climate of ambivalence among project dwellers. Nonetheless, most women in public housing did seek out and establish a few guarded interpersonal associations with nearby residents, tentative as many of them were.

Table 4-1 shows the relationship between interracial project neighboring and racial prejudice for the respondents who resided in desegregated projects.[a] The

---

[a]The analysis includes the 33 respondents who comprised the minority element in projects having a large majority of the other race. The housewives living in segregated projects were excluded. In other words, the 102 respondents represent all the women living in projects wherein interracial neighboring was possible.

data generally support the hypothesis that housewives who engage in interracial neighboring tend to be less prejudiced than women who do little or no interracial neighboring. However, the strength of the association is quite different for black and white respondents. There is a strong association $(G = 0.75)$[b] between the presence of interracial neighboring and a lesser degree of racial prejudice for white housewives. In contrast, although the association between interracial neighboring and prejudice is in the hypothesized direction for blacks, it is not statistically significant ($p > 0.05$).

It is evident that knowing whether or not white housewives neighbor with black project residents improves prediction[c] of the degree of their racial prejudice; the more a white respondent engages in interracial neighboring the less prejudiced she is likely to be. Differences in the degree of interracial neighboring do not explain the variation in prejudice for black respondents as well as they do for whites. For example, 45 percent (eighteen) of the black housewives reported minimal prejudice and did not engage in interracial neighboring. Black housewives, irrespective of their neighboring behavior, were less prejudiced than whites.

We turn now to the relationship between interracial neighboring and the way respondents perceived the position held by their reference groups on the issue of residential desegregation (table 4-2). The patterns of relationship in these data are quite similar to those in the preceding analysis. However, when black and white residents are considered together, the association between neighboring and perceiving reference groups as tolerant of desegregation is not statistically significant.

Again there is considerable difference between the amount of explained variation when this relationship is examined separately for blacks and whites. Among the white respondents there is a strongly positive and significant relationship between neighboring with black project dwellers and perceiving one's reference groups as favoring racial desegregation in housing. Although the association between these variables for the black respondents is in the direction hypothesized ($G = 0.18$), a knowledge of interracial neighboring is a far less effective predictor of perceived reference group position than it is for white respondents.

---

[b]The coefficient of rank association (Gamma) is a nonparametric measure, varying between -1.0 and +1.0; it has its own test of significance which was used throughout the analysis. See Linton C. Freeman, *Elementary Applied Statistics* (New York: John Wiley, 1965), pp. 170-174.

---

[c]Gamma is one of the "proportional reduction in error" measures of ordinal association. As such, its values indicate the degree to which one's rank in terms of one variable is predictable from a knowledge of his rank on another variable. It is in this sense that "prediction" should be interpreted.

Table 4-1
Interracial Neighboring Contacts and Degree of Racial Prejudice, by Race

| | Neighboring Contacts | | | | | | | |
| | White Housewives[a] | | | | Black Housewives[b] | | | |
Racial Prejudice	Many	Several	Few/None	Totals	Many	Several	Few/None	Totals
Low	7	4	3	14	2	4	18	24
Moderate	1	8	9	18	4	0	12	16
High	0	2	16	18	1	1	10	12
Totals	8	14	28	50	7	5	40	52

(Total N = 102)

[a]Gamma = 0.75 $p < .01$
[b]Gamma = 0.08 N.S.

Note: Gamma (both groups combined) = 0.43 $p < 0.01$

Table 4-2
Interracial Neighboring Contacts and Housewives' Perceptions of Their Reference Groups' Attitude toward Desegregation, by Race

Reference Groups perceived as:	Neighboring Contacts							
	White Housewives[a]				Black Housewives[b]			
	Many	Several	Few/None	Totals	Many	Several	Few/None	Totals
Tolerant	4	1	0	5	4	3	25	32
Mixed feelings	4	8	9	21	1	1	9	11
Opposed	0	5	17	22	0	0	1	1
Totals	8	14	26	48	5	4	35	44

(Total N = 92)[c]

[a]Gamma = 0.78 $p < .01$

[b]Gamma = 0.18 N.S.

[c]Ten cases are excluded from analysis due to insufficient data on reference groups.

Note: Gamma (both groups combined) = 0.17 N.S.

The data in tables 4-1 and 4-2 clearly illustrate that differences in the degree of interracial neighboring do not explain the variation in either racial prejudice or perception of "significant others' " position on desegregation for black respondents as well as they do for white respondents. Black women, regardless of whether they neighbor with white residents, tend to hold less racial prejudice and more often perceive their reference groups as tolerant of desegregation than white housewives. For blacks, while the associations between interracial neighboring and the two dependent variables are in the direction of the hypothesis, they are not statistically significant, and, therefore, the research hypothesis must be held in question. On the other hand, the research hypothesis is supported for the white respondents.

Previous Equal-Status Contact

A second important independent variable in the study was the amount of equal-status contacts respondents experienced with members of the other race prior to entering public housing. In table 4-3 the results of the analysis examining the relationship between these previous contacts and the degree of respondents' racial prejudice are presented. The findings affirm the hypothesized relationship that the greater the amount of previous equal-status contact, the less racial prejudice is manifested. The strength of the relationship is strong and statistically significant ($p < 0.01$) for both racial groups taken together as well as for each viewed separately, although more variation in prejudice is accounted for by a knowledge of previous contacts among white respondents ($G = 0.72$) than it is for black housewives ($G = 0.43$). Even though previous contact is a better predictor of degree of prejudice for white respondents than it is for blacks, examinaiton of table 4-3 shows few "deviant cases" for black respondents. Only one black women who had minimal prejudice had few previous equal-status contacts, and only four (12 percent) prejudiced blacks had many previous interracial contacts that were of an equalitarian nature. We suggest that the reason blacks report more previous interracial contacts than their white counterparts is largely due to the fact that black respondents were somewhat younger than whites and they had been reared in an urban environment in contrast to a rural setting, thereby affording them more opportunities than white respondents to enter into equal-status associations.

Table 4-4 presents the correspondence between respondents' previous equal-status contacts and their perception of their reference groups' position on residential desegregation. It is immediately apparent that previous equal-status contacts with members of the other race is a good predictor of perceived reference group tolerance of desegregation among white respondents ($G = 0.75$, $p < 0.01$), but that for blacks the research hypothesis finds no support. In fact, there is a slight inverse relationship between the extent of previous contacts and perceiving reference groups' position as tolerant. Among black respondents there

Table 4-3
Previous Interracial Equal-Status Contacts and Degree of Racial Prejudice, by Race

	Previous Contacts							
Racial Prejudice	White Housewives[a]				Black Housewives[b]			
	Many	Several	Few/None	Totals	Many	Several	Few/None	Totals
Low	6	12	0	18	22	17	1	40
Moderate	5	21	1	27	7	16	6	29
High	3	18	17	38	4	9	1	14
Totals	14	51	18	83	33	42	8	83

(Total N = 166)[c]

[a]Gamma = 0.72 $p < 0.01$

[b]Gamma = 0.43 $p < 0.01$

[c]There was no composite prejudice score for two housewives.

Note: Gamma (both groups combined) = 0.59 $p < 0.01$

is comparatively little variability regarding the way in which they perceive their reference groups — fifty-one women (77 percent) believe they would be tolerant of desegregation, fourteen (21 percent) are uncertain, and only one housewife believed her reference groups were apposed to residential desegregation.

The evidence in tables 4-3 and 4-4 clearly substantiates the research hypothesis regarding previous interracial contacts and both racial prejudice and perception of reference groups' position among the white respondents. Less variation in prejudice is accounted for among blacks by these prior contacts than among whites, but the relationship is statistically significant for this group of respondents as well and thus supports the research hypothesis. The unexpected slightly negative association between previous equal-status relationships and perception of reference groups position for blacks is probably largely a product of the lack of variability of perception among these respondents; the vast majority of black housewives perceived their reference groups as being tolerant of residential desegregation. Whatever the explanation, this particular research hypothesis finds no support among black respondents.

Duration of Residence

Table 4-5 presents a test of the hypothesis that housewives who live in a desegregated project for a longer period of time will be less prejudiced than newcomers to the project. Contrary to what was hypothesized, the data suggest that black housewives who lived in desegregated housing for the longest period of time were more likely to hold intolerant racial attitudes and for white women, duration explained little of the variation in prejudice. This inverse relationship is shown in the table for black housewives (G = -0.37); the research hypothesis is plainly unsupported for these respondents. There would appear to have been nothing about a long duration of residence in desegregated housing that was conducive to tolerant interracial attitudes for these women. Twenty percent (seven) of the black housewives who lived in the John Harrison (desegregated) project were highly prejudiced toward whites and all had lived in that project for more than six months — none were newcomers.

A different relationship is depicted between duration of residence and racial attitude among white housewives. The association for these respondents is in the direction hypothesized, but it is not of sufficient strength to be statistically significant ($p > 0.05$, < 0.10). Therefore, the evidence pertaining to this hypothesis for white respondents must be considered inconclusive. Despite the fact that all whites harboring minimal racial prejudice were "long-time" residents of the project, a majority of white respondents having moderate and high prejudices toward blacks also had lived in the project for more than a year. Put in another way, relatively little variation in racial prejudice is explained by duration of residence.

With regard to the relationship between duration of residence and perception

Table 4-4
Previous Interracial Equal-Status Contacts and Housewives' Perceptions of Their Reference Groups' Attitude toward Desegregation, by Race

| Reference Groups Perceived as: | Previous Contacts | | | | | | | |
| | White Housewives[a] | | | | Black Housewives[b] | | | |
	Many	Several	Few/None	Totals	Many	Several	Few/None	Totals
Tolerant	5	1	0	6	21	25	5	51
Mixed feelings	4	21	3	28	8	6	0	14
Opposed	3	26	13	42	0	0	1	1
Totals	12	48	16	76	29	31	6	66

(Total N = 142)[c]

[a]Gamma = 0.75 $p < .01$

[b]Gamma = −0.18 N.S.

[c]Twenty-six cases are excluded from analysis due to insufficient data on reference groups.

Note: Gamma (both groups combined) = 0.55 $p < 0.01$

Table 4-5
Duration of Residence in Desegregated Project and Degree of Racial Prejudice, by Race

Duration of Residence

Racial Prejudice	White Housewives[a]				Black Housewives[b]			
	More Than One Year	Seven Months to One Year	Six Months or Less	Totals	More Than One Year	Seven Months to One Year	Six Months or Less	Totals
Low	5	0	0	5	6	5	5	16
Moderate	13	2	1	16	6	5	1	12
High	11	1	1	13	4	3	0	7
Totals	29	3	2	34	16	13	6	35

(Total N = 69)

[a] Gamma = 0.22 N.S. ($\rho > .05$)
[b] Gamma = −0.37

Note: Gamma (both groups combined) = −0.33

of reference groups' position on desegregation, table 4-6 shows an association clearly contrary to that which was hypothesized. Long duration of residence in the racially desegregated project is not positively related to a perception that reference groups are tolerant of residential desegregation among housewives of either race. In fact, the obverse appears to be the case, as suggested by the negative Gamma coefficients; duration of residence tends to be related to perception of reference groups, but in the opposite direction to that of the research hypothesis.

Summarizing the data pertaining to duration of residence within the desegregated housing project, it appears that the length of time respondents lived in that environment is not directly related to greater racial tolerance. The data suggest that it was the black housewives who had resided in the desegregated project longest who were the most intolerant, and who perceived their reference groups as sanctioning segregation. For white housewives, little variation in racial prejudice is explained by their length of residence in the project, and the longer they resided therein the more likely they are to see their reference groups as opposed to residential desegregation. On the basis of the data analysis, the research hypotheses concerning duration of residence cannot be upheld. We will return to a discussion of the apparent "negative" effects of the duration in the following chapters.

Race As a Proxy

Table 4-7 demonstrates that there is a strong positive and statistically significant association between being black and both holding racially tolerant attitudes and perceiving one's reference groups' as favoring residential desegregation. The results are not surprising; the reader has recognized from the preceding tabular analyses that it appeared that black respondents were less prejudiced toward whites than whites were toward blacks, and that blacks are more inclined than are whites to view their reference groups as holding more tolerant positions regarding desegregation. The table documents the fact that blacks demonstrate greater interracial tolerance than their white counterparts who live in the same desegregated environment.[d]

Part of the general hypothesis states that racial tolerance is positively associated with a lack of perceived status threat from living in a racially desegregated environment. Generally, in terms of our test of the contact hypothesis, race is conceived of as an antecedent control variable. However, in this instance, race serves as a proxy for the degree of status threat. An examination of the relationship between race and the two dependent variables

---

[d]Again, it should be kept in mind that it is contact and not the occupancy pattern per se that is treated as the independent variable. The occupancy pattern (desegregated, segregated) of the projects was not significantly related to either attitudes or perceptions. For example, living in a desegregated project is not related to more tolerant attitudes.

Table 4-6
Duration of Residence in a Desegregated Project and Housewives' Perceptions of Their Reference Groups' Attitude toward Desegregation, by Race

Duration of Residence

Reference Groups Perceived as:	White Housewives[a]				Black Housewives[b]			
	More Than One Year	Seven Months to One Year	Six Months or Less	Totals	More Than One Year	Seven Months to One Year	Six Months or Less	Totals
Tolerant	0	0	0	0	6	9	3	18
Mixed feelings	12	1	2	15	7	1	2	10
Opposed	16	2	0	18	0	1	0	1
Totals	28	3	2	33	13	11	5	29

(Total N = 62)[c]

[a]Gamma = −0.37 N.S.

[b]Gamma = −0.30 N.S.

[c]Seven cases are excluded from analysis due to insufficient data on reference groups.

Note: Gamma (both groups combined) = −0.57 N.S.

Table 4-7

The Race of Housewives in Desegregated Public Housing: Their Racial Prejudice and Perceptions of Reference Groups' Position on Residential Desegregation

Racial Prejudice	Race		
	Black	White	
Low	16	5	
Moderate	12	16	
High	7	13	
No. of respondents	35	34	N = 69

Note: Gamma = 0.51 $\rho < .01$

Reference Groups Perceived as:	Race		
	Black	White	
Favorable	18	0	
Mixed feelings	10	15	
Opposed	1	18	
No. of respondents	29	33	N = 62[a]

[a]Seven cases excluded from analysis due to insufficient data on housewife's reference groups.

Note: Gamma = 0.96 $\rho < .01$

(prejudice and perception of reference group), therefore, should be interpreted as an indirect indicator of felt status threat or enhancement. In this regard, table 4-7 provides an indirect test of the proposition that residential desegregation poses considerable status threat to white residents while posing comparatively little threat to their black counterparts. It is this proposition that is supported by the strength of the associations and their statistical significance.

A Resident Inventory of Interracial Experience

In order to provide a more comprehensive measure of the contact hypothesis within the research context, an effort was made to measure the combined effect of four variables upon racial prejudice and perception of reference groups. Those four variables were interracial neighboring, interracial contacts implying social equality made prior to moving into public housing, living in a desegregated project, and living in a desegregated project for a "long" period of time (a year or more). During the coding procedure and prior to analysis, each respondent was classified according to whether or not she had been exposed to each of these four life experiences. A respondent could have had all these experiences, none, or any possible combination — twelve in all.

Table 4-8 should be interpreted as a tabular formulation of the hypothesis stating that as respondents' degree of exposure to equal-status interracial contacts declines there will be a corresponding decline in their racial tolerance and the extent to which they view their reference groups as being tolerant of desegregation.[e] Each respondent was placed in one of the twelve categories shown in table 4-8. Respondents in category I engaged in interracial neighboring, experienced previous equal-status interracial contact, were residing in a desegregated project, and had lived there for more than a year. They represent tenants who had maximum equal-status exposure to members of the other race, as measured by these particular variables. Each successive category (II-XII) represents a decreasing degree of interracial equal-status experience. It was hypothesized that women in category I would hold more tolerant attitudes and perceive greater tolerance on the behalf of their reference groups than those in categories II, III, IV, etc. In category XII we would expect to find those housewives with the least tolerant attitudes and the perceptions of the greatest amount of opposition to desegregation.

Each of the four variables used in this composite inventory was dichotomized; every respondent was classified as either having the attribute in question or not. She either neighbored with members of the other race or did not, had some previous interracial contacts or did not, etc. The variables are entered in table 4-8, from left to right, in descending order of the degree of influence they bring to bear on individuals' attitudes and perceptions.

The data in table 4-9 show the degree to which residents' combined interracial experiences account for variation in their racial prejudices. The numbers entered in the body of the table indicate the number of respondents. Expectations concerning the relationship between contact experience and prejudice are substantiated for both racial groups taken together and especially for white housewives. However, when blacks are analyzed separately, the hypothesis is unsupported. Findings for white respondents, in contrast, show a strong and statistically significant association ($G = 0.62, p < 0.01$). Examination of table 4-9 shows few inversions for the white group, where as inversions for black respondents are frequent. There is a strong ordinal association among white housewives between the degree of exposure to equal-status experiences with blacks and less racial antipathy. On the other hand, a knowledge of black

---

[e]Assumptions were made concerning the comparative importance of the four variables in predicting the intensity of racial prejudice. The two variables which actually measure equal-status contact (neighboring and previous contact) were considered to have more predictive power than were the two variables reflecting exposure to desegregated living (residing in a desegregated project and duration of residence). Engaging in interracial neighboring, because of its immediacy and relatively close nature, was assumed to be slightly more important than previous equal-status contact. Residing in desegregated housing was assumed to be more important than duration of residence. Thus the four variables were ranked in the following order, according to their assumed strength as predictors of prejudice and perception: interracial neighboring, previous equal-status contact, residence in a desegregated project, and long duration of residence in a desegregated project.

Table 4-8
Hypothesized Relationship between Resident Type Defined by Different Levels of Interracial Contact and Racial Prejudice and Perception[a]

Residents' Contact Profile	Behavioral-Environmental Variables				Ordered Racial Attitudes and Reference Group Perception: Tolerant to Intolerant
	Interracial Neighboring	Equal-Status Previous Contacts	Desegregated Project	"Long" Residence	
I	X	X	X	X	1
II	X	X	X	O	2
III	X	O	X	X	3
IV	X	O	X	O	4
V	O	X	X	X	5
VI	O	X	O	O	6
VII	O	X	O	O	7
VIII	O	O	X	X	8
IX	O	O	X	X	9
X	O	O	O	O	10
XI[b]	O	O	O	O	11
XII	O	O	O	X	12

[a]X indicates that these attributes pertain to the category, and O indicates that they do not.

[b]Categories XI and XII appear reversed, in terms of the logic of sequence. However, a "long" residence in a segregated environment (XII) is reasoned to be more likely associated with negative interracial feelings than a short residence in the same environment.

Table 4-9

Number of Housewives in Each of Twelve Categories of Degree of Equal-Status Contact, Subclassified by Race and by Prejudice

White Housewives

Type Respondent According to Interracial Contact Experience

Racial Prejudice	I	II	III	IV	V	VI	VII	VIII	IX	X	XI	XII	Total
Low	5	8	0	1	0	0	1	3	0	0	0	0	18
Moderate	7	4	2	0	1	1	3	5	3	0	1	0	27
High	1	2	0	4	2	0	4	4	8	1	2	10	38
Totals	13	14	2	5	3	1	8	12	11	1	3	10	83

Note: Gamma = 0.62 $p < 0.01$

Black Housewives

Racial Prejudice	I	II	III	IV	V	VI	VII	VIII	IX	X	XI	XII	Total
Low	5	7	0	1	3	8	6	9	0	0	0	1	40
Moderate	5	5	0	0	1	3	1	7	1	1	0	5	29
High	2	1	0	0	4	3	0	2	0	2	0	0	14
Totals	12	13	0	1	8	14	7	18	1	3	0	6	83

(Total N = 166)[a]

aNo composite prejudice score for two housewives.

bGamma (both groups combined) = 0.38 $p < 0.01$

Note: Gamma = 0.03 N.S.

respondents' interracial inventory is ineffective in predicting their degree of prejudice.

Turning to the relationship between interracial experience and perception of reference group position, table 4-10 shows support for the hypothesis for white respondents but not for blacks. The direction of the relationship for blacks is the reverse of that predicted — perceiving one's reference groups as being tolerant of residential desegregation tends to be associated with fewer equal-status contacts with whites! Those equal-status experiences for which we have data are not associated with perceptions of reference groups in the hypothesized direction for black housewives, and therefore, the contact hypothesis is not supported in this instance.

Housewives Assess Their Own Attitude Change

Early in the interviews, prior to administering the attitude scale items and the reference group inventory, the respondents were asked to report how they perceived their interracial attitudes had changed as a result of living in the public housing projects. Table 4-11 shows their responses by project and race. Not unexpectedly, a majority of housewives reported they experienced no change in their interracial feelings after entering the projects. This was particularly true of black residents in the segregated project. A large minority of respondents from each of the other remaining types of projects did report a change in their racial views. Interestingly, both black and white women in desegregated projects more frequently reported that their outlook toward members of the other race became *more* favorable as opposed to less favorable after living in public housing. This was particularly true of black women; more than four times the number of these respondents reported a favorable attitude change as those reporting an unfavorable change. Perhaps the most interesting contrast is that between the self-reports of whites in the segregated project and those in desegregated projects. Forty-two percent of the white housewives in the segregated project claimed that their attitudes toward blacks had become *less* favorable since moving to public housing, whereas only 14 percent of the white respondents in desegregated housing reported that their attitudes had changed in this direction. Once again it would appear as if the threat of a "Negro invasion" precipitated more negative feelings toward blacks than did actually residing in a desegregated project.

Interracial Neighboring and Different Dimensions of Racial Prejudice

In this last section of the chapter, data are presented to test the hypothesis that respondents living in the same project and neighboring with members of the

Table 4-10
Number of Housewives in Each of Twelve Categories of Degree of Equal-Status Contact, Subclassified by Race and by Reference Groups' Attitude toward Desegregation

White Housewives

Reference Groups Perceived as:	Type Respondent According to Interracial Contact Experience												
	I	II	III	IV	V	VI	VII	VIII	IX	X	XI	XII	Total
Tolerant	0	5	0	0	0	0	1	0	0	0	0	0	6
Mixed feelings	8	6	1	2	1	1	1	5	2	0	1	0	28
Opposed	5	3	1	2	2	0	4	7	8	1	1	8	42
Totals	13	14	2	4	3	1	6	12	10	1	2	8	76

Note: Gamma = 0.50 $p < 0.01$

Black Housewives

Reference Groups Perceived as:	I	II	III	IV	V	VI	VII	VIII	IX	X	XI	XII	Total
Tolerant	6	8	0	0	5	11	3	13	1	1	0	3	51
Mixed feelings	4	2	0	1	2	2	2	1	0	0	0	0	14
Opposed	0	0	0	0	0	0	0	0	0	1	0	0	1
Totals	10	10	0	1	7	13	5	14	1	2	0	3	66

Note: Gamma = -0.28 N.S.

(Total N = 142)

aTwenty-six cases are excluded from analysis due to insufficient data on reference groups.
bGamma (both groups combined) = 0.19 $p < 0.05$

Table 4-11
Housewife's Self-Reported Attitude Change toward Members of the Other Race after Entering Public Housing

Her attitude . . .	Type Project and Race			
	Segregated Black (percentage)	Desegregated Black (percentage)	Segregated White (percentage)	Desegregated White (percentage)
Did not change	88	56	58	62
Became less favorable	6	8	42	14
Became more favorable	3	34	0	22
No response	3	2	0	2
	100	100	100	100
	(N = 33)	(N = 52)	(N = 33)	(N = 50)

other race will be less intolerant in terms of the residential dimension of racial prejudice than on any one of the other dimensions measured.[f] Recall that the social distance scale used to provide an overall measure of racial prejudice was comprised of four separate scales, each measuring a different dimension of prejudice: residential prejudice, positional prejudice, interpersonal-physical prejudice, and interpersonal-social prejudice. The comparative intensity of racial prejudice on four distinctive dimensions is examined in table 4-12.

Table 4-12 shows the number of respondents manifesting "high" and "low" degrees of racial prejudice on each of the four dimensions for the fifty-nine housewives who resided in desegregated projects and reported at least a minimum of interracial neighboring. High and low prejudice were simply designated as those above and below the median prejudice score for each dimension. The difference of proportions test was employed to indicate the extent of differences between dimensions of prejudice.

The data generally support the hypothesis; however, the evidence must remain somewhat inconclusive because the differences between dimensions tend to be small. Whereas white housewives were clearly more tolerant on the residential dimension of prejudice than on either the positional or interpersonal-physical dimensions, they were slightly more tolerant on the interpersonal-social dimension than on the residential. Put in another way, white housewives objected less to living in the same project with blacks than they did to having physical contact with blacks. They objected *most* to affording blacks positions of social and political influence. These white housewives were slightly more willing to relate to blacks in a friendly, informal manner (visiting) than they were toward having them live next door!

The data for black respondents support the hypothesis more conclusively: blacks showed less prejudice on the residential dimension than on any other. In contrast to white housewives, who appeared least tolerant on the positional dimension of prejudice, black women showed least tolerance on the interpersonal-social dimension — the dimension on which their white counterparts were most tolerant! Black women were most reluctant to have "friendship" relations with whites and least intolerant with respect to living in the same neighborhood. Examination of table 4-12 also shows that black respondents were less prejudiced than whites on all dimensions except the dimension of interpersonal-social prejudice.

Before summarizing the general findings, discussing their implications and suggesting alternate interpretations, we turn first to special consideration of the reaction of black housewives to equal-status contact.

---

[f]The reader may wish to refer to chapter 1's subsection, "Dimensions of Prejudice," for the related theoretical discussion.

Table 4-12
Levels of Prejudice on Four Dimensions among Black and White Housewives[a] Engaging in Interracial Neighboring within Desegregated Projects

Degree of Racial Prejudice	Type Project and Race			
	Residential Prejudice	Positional Prejudice	Interpersonal-Physical Prejudice	Interpersonal-Social Prejudice
Low (below median)				
White	23 (67.6%)	12 (35.3%)	18 (52.9%)	26 (76.5%)
Black	21 (84.0%)	19 (76.0%)	18 (72.0%)	17 (68.0%)
Both	44 (74.6%)	31 (52.5%)	36 (61.0%)	43 (72.8%)
High (above median)				
White	11 (32.4%)	22 (64.7%)	16 (47.1%)	8 (23.5%)
Black	4 (16.0%)	6 (24.0%)	7 (28.0%)	8 (32.0%)
Both	15 (25.4%)	28 (47.5%)	23 (39.0%)	16 (27.2%)

[a]White housewives (N = 34); Black housewives (N = 25); both groups combined (N = 59).

Difference of Proportions:

Residential with Positional

White: $p < 0.01$
Black: $p < 0.10$
Both: $p < 0.01$

Residential with Physical

$p < 0.10$
$p < 0.05$
$p < 0.06$

Residential with Social

N.S.
$p < 0.01$
N.S.

5 The Black Response

The principal hypothesis of this study was that there exists a positive relationship between equal-status interracial contact and racial tolerance. The analysis presented in the preceding chapter supported the contact hypothesis as it applied to the white respondents, but unlike the reported findings of earlier studies,[1] the proposition was only partially, and inconclusively, confirmed for the black respondents. This chapter gives special attention to the reactions of black housewives who lived in a formerly all-white housing project and who were labeled "invaders" by many white residents and some Housing Authority personnel. Emphasis is placed upon the meaning that such equal-status contacts have for blacks.

Whereas we were not surprised to find a dissimilarity between the black and white responses to contact and to desegregation, certain findings for the black respondents appear inconsistent with the theoretical rationale of the contact hypothesis and warrent closer inspection. Looking only at the response of the black housewives, we see that there are essentially two instances where the results are contrary to expectations. First, although the relationship appeared to be in the direction hypothesized, interpersonal neighborly contact with white project dwellers was not significantly related to reduced prejudice or to the perception that one's reference groups were tolerant of desegregation. Second, according to the measures used, it appeared that "long-time" black residents in desegregated projects were the most prejudiced and were more likely to see their reference groups as undecided rather than approving on the issue of residential desegregation.

Black Women View "Equal-Status" Contacts

With regard to the first of these contradictory results, the inconclusive findings for black women were very likely a partial function of the comparative lack of variability in neighboring.[a] Black housewives reported considerably fewer interracial neighboring contacts than whites. Examination of interviews indicated no evidence that whites were neighboring with a comparatively few interracially oriented blacks! Whereas there were a number of pairs of

[a]There was also less variability for black respondents with regard to the two dependent variables. For the black respondents in this study, the scale items do not discriminate as effectively between degrees of prejudice as they do for whites.

black-white neighbors who were reasonably close, there were no black women who were socially intimate with more than one white housewife. Analysis revealed that it was the white woman who most often initiated interpersonal relationships, which by virtue of the measure of interracial neighboring used, increased their scores as compared to their black counterparts. We feel, however, that aside from issues of measurement, the findings also suggest that it would be useful to explore how blacks interpret those interracial contacts we call equal-status within the context of the study.

Although the contact hypothesis should be theoretically applicable for the minority group as well as the dominant group, this generalization is founded upon studies of the effect relatively sustained and equalitarian interpersonal contact has upon the racial attitudes of white respondents. The few studies which have addressed themselves to the effects these contacts have upon blacks,[2] leave the reader with the impression that the same process of attitudinal change occurs for blacks as for whites upon entering into equal-status exchanges. Given our knowledge of the differential life experiences by race, it should appear naive to assume that black reactions to interpersonal contacts with whites are the mirror image of those of their white counterpart. It is highly unlikely that the same equal-status contacts are similarly perceived and interpreted by blacks and whites. Whereas it is possible to define what kind of interracial associations can be referred to as "objectively" equal-status in nature, it is the meaning such contacts have for the individual that is most important. The interviews showed that black and white respondents entered into neighborly relations with one another with very different anticipations and anxieties.

The black women in this study brought to any equal-status relationships they had with white neighbors a considerably different set of life experiences than those of their white neighbors. Of the two groups, it was the black women who were the "experts" on race relations. They were cognizant of the subtle nuances of dominant-subordinant relationships and nearly all had been previously subjected to rebuff and unpleasantries at the hands of whites. As Johnson suggests, because of such experiences, blacks learn to be suspect of *any* relationships with whites — even those which do not openly suggest differential status.[3] In other words, blacks learn to "keep up their guard." This defensive posture was well illustrated by one middle-aged housewife who commented:

I tell my kids to be pleasant to the white folks here but not to get involved — that's dangerous! I know, I've been burned before. Whenever trouble stirs between whites and us, you know its going to be the Negro who loses. There's lots of us in the projects, but you know the color of the face behind the desk! (referring to the Housing Authority office)

This reserve which was shared by a great many black women should not be interpreted as an excessively submissive attitude. In the Border City projects, black women were quick to perceive condescending attitudes on the part of their white neighbors, even if these were not recognized by the whites to whom they were relating. These patronizing white neighbors were resented by black women nearly as much as whites who deliberately ignored blacks and members of their families. It was this kind of reserve and suspicion that resulted in black respondents being slightly more intolerant of whites on the interpersonal-social dimension of prejudice than on any other dimension (chapter 4). Of course, such an approach to relations with members of the other race could be expected in public housing wherein there was widespread tenant dissatisfaction.

Despite the fact that black women approached interracial contact with caution and hesitancy, the majority of these housewives were in favor of desegregated living. This position was not necessarily the result of actual contact with tolerant whites within the project, and it was certainly not due to any desire for interracial contact per se. These women favored desegregated life because they felt that it would ultimately offer more advantages and a healthier physical environment for them and especially for their children. For example, one black housewife and mother had this to say of racial desegregation:

It's best for the kids. When they see what whites are doing and how they're doing it, they will do better. It's the only way our people are going to get more out of life. We'll have to get in with them.

This black view of those contacts we have termed equal-status, especially when contrasted with the white response presented in the next chapter, helps explain why the net effect of such interracial contact upon blacks is not a reduction of prejudice comparable to that found for white respondents.

The reader should not interpret the prevasive black approval of desegregation as an indication that these women were "whitewardly" oriented. While there was no widespread sentiment for black identity as we currently know it among project housewives, neither was there any indication that these respondents were ashamed of their race. In fact, what appeared to take place as a result of living in close proximity to lower-income whites was an enhancement of self-esteem among quite a number of black housewives and their families. One black housewife expressed this feeling as follows:

They [white residents] have no right to feel better than us — who do they think they are? Some of them are just poor folks like us, but others are nothing but trash. We've got no reason to be lappin' all over them!

The "Invaders' " Viewpoint

We turn now to the second set of findings for black respondents that was counter to what had been hypothesized — the fact that duration within the desegregated housing project was not positively related to either racially tolerant attitudes or to the perception of one's reference groups as favoring residential desegregation. Originally, we argued that the opportunity to engage in interracial contacts within the desegregated project would increase with the duration of residence. Again, recall that it was not the desegregated occupancy pattern of the project which was hypothesized to affect prejudice and perceptions. Upon closer examination of what took place, it became clear that duration of residence became associated with other factors. Whereas these factors were related to the lack of relationship between duration and tolerance for white respondents, they were, in conjunction with certain other aspects of race relations, responsible for the fact that those black housewives who had resided in desegregated housing for greater lengths of time tended to be *less* tolerant.

What occurred with respect to duration of residence for many project housewives was the following. As we have seen, the most prevalent sources of tenant discontent were a felt lack of privacy, a lack of discipline among young children, a high rate of delinquency among neighborhood teenagers, undue surveillance by the Housing Authority, and a lack of adequate project maintenance and repair. Because so many incoming project dwellers came from homes with serious inadequacies, the project apartments with their convenient facilities and relatively inexpensive rents were welcomed — especially after the typical long wait families had to undergo before moving into the projects. The improvement in the living quarters remained a source of gratification for several months for most newcomers, but after living in the projects beyond that, the above sources of discontent became increasing salient. As other researchers have discovered in other low-income projects, it is at this stage that many residents become resigned to the fact that their lot has not improved substantially, if indeed it has not become worse in some respects.[4] This routinized discontent and frustration is essentially the same as that which Coser reported was typically found among welfare recipients.[5] This attitude is exemplified by the comment of a black housewife in her second year of project living:

Everyone is in too close here — it gets to you after awhile. The walls are so thin it sounds like your neighbors are in the next room.[b] I guess I shouldn't complain more than the others . . . but I can't see how some take it year by year.

This disillusionment with project life took place earlier for many black housewives who were cast in the role of "invaders" by many whites in the project. It is important to remember that the housing project labeled desegregated had undergone a period of exceedingly rapid transition; this project had only two years previously been solely occupied by white families. The response of black residents must be understood not only in terms of their view

---

[b]The complaint that apartment walls were too thin was one voiced by a great many tenants. Having seen many of the former dwellings of project tenants, we find it difficult to believe that they were less susceptible to the infiltration of noise. The complaint would appear to be part of a syndrome manifest together with a number of related frustrations. And, the noise in and around apartment buildings undoubtedly became more frustrating due to the fact that upon entering the projects many women spent increasing amounts of time within the home, as we have noted earlier.

of project life in contrast to that outside the projects, but also as a reaction to the behavior of white project residents. Whites, here designated as long-time occupants, had witnessed a rapid influx of blacks in "their" project, whereas the long-time black residents were among the first of their race to enter this formerly segregated project. Among a number of these white families, there was marked resentment concerning the "Negro invasion," which is discussed in additional detail in chapter 6. Here, it is sufficient to indicate that this resentment was communicated to a number of the black respondents.

Black women who had been among the first families to "desegregate" the project and who had lived there the longest expressed resentment concerning the treatment afforded them by whites. In the course of the interviews, it became clear that these women objected to the lack of social recognition and the contentious attitudes some of their white neighbors held toward them and the members of their families.[c] These women also suffered from feeling comparatively isolated from other black women among whom they felt more comfortable and with whom they could more readily establish neighborly relations — relations which could help alleviate loneliness and the perceived indignities. Under the circumstances of "involuntary" biracial propinquity, black housewives and their families who entered the project early were cast in the roles of intruders which resulted in a different but equally stressful challenge than the one perceived by white residents.[6] One of these housewives expressed herself this way:

When I came, I was the first Negro in these buildings and did I get a hard time from some of the whites. Every time I'd have friends over, they'd [next door neighbors] call the police. And they've got six noisy kids! They [many whites in the project] wouldn't even say hello or nod their heads — except maybe at the bus stop when they was standing there for a while trying not to notice me.

Another black respondent said:

You'd have thought that we asked to live next door so we could rub off on them [whites] or something. I don't like it any better than they do. We're all here because we don't have another place to go and that don't make them any better than us.

It appears that the evidence did not convincingly bear out the contact hypothesis for the black respondents due to the fact that many had to assume the burden of being the "invader" and particularly because the affect of these

---

[c]Five black housewives who had lived in the project for more than a year voiced resentment concerning the treatment they received by staff members of the Housing Authority upon entering the then nearly all white project. They claimed that they were advised, in subtle and not so subtle terms, that they would have to be exceptionally "good Negroes" because they were moving into a "white" project.

equal-status contacts varied with race.[d] Regular and relatively "friendly" contacts with black status peers apparently undermined negative racial stereotypes to the degree necessary to result in a change in whites' racial attitudes. The racial stereotype held by whites was largely based on a characterization of blacks as being different kinds of individuals — a vulnerable characterization in the presence of informal interracial relationships. On the other hand, blacks generally viewed whites not so much as individuals incapable of behaving differently, but more as persons predisposed to unjust treatment of blacks. A change in this kind of perspective requires a more intensive relationship between blacks and whites — a relationship which is, for the most part, different from those contacts reported in this study. The very same contacts which served to lessen whites' prejudices had considerably less effect upon the interracial attitudes of the black residents whose attitudes toward contact were initially more tolerant. Biracial proximity did not present as great a threat to blacks as it did to whites. What many black housewives came to resent in desegregated housing was behavior on the part of their white neighbors which implied that they were anything less than their status equals in a situation where they knew this was not or should not be the case.

---

[d]Table 4-11 reported that 34 percent of blacks in desegregated projects reported that their attitude toward whites had improved after entering public housing; this is a greater proportion reporting an attitude change in this direction than for whites in desegregated projects! Further analysis showed that a disproportionate number of less tolerant blacks reported no change in attitude (56 percent) and that a sizeable number of these were newcomers to the Green Tree West (predominantly white) project. Those long-term residents who constituted the minority that reported their interracial attitudes became more favorable represent an interesting case: they apparently felt more tolerant of whites as increasing numbers of blacks entered the project.

6

The Situational Approach to Contact: Further Interpretations and Conclusions

In this the final chapter we turn to a look at the white response in order to round out the discussion found in the preceding chapter, address the issue of tenant selectivity by initial interracial attitudes, and conclude with a presentation of the results as viewed from a situational perspective.

The White Response

Confirmation under Unfavorable Circumstances

Previous analysis has shown that the contact hypothesis was rather convincingly supported within the research context for white housewives who lived in the Border City public housing projects. These results add support to the body of research literature which has examined the effects of equal-status interracial contact upon white respondents. The results must be considered somewhat surprising given the generally unfavorable circumstances within which the residential desegregation and interracial contact occurred. In fact, the social climate within the public housing projects was far from that which one would expect to enhance friendly neighboring relations among members of the same race far less between the races. It has been shown elsewhere that the resistance of whites to desegregation and to contact with minority group members is increased when the incoming nonwhite group is large and threatens to become the majority.[1] In the case of the desegregated project studied here black residents had very rapidly become the numerical majority.

Within desegregated housing, a number of white housewives avoided their black neighbors, while others refused to relate to blacks as status equals and/or failed to perceive the implied symbolic equality of sharing a neighborhood or the social equality of interracial neighboring. However, the contact hypothesis gained support by virtue of the number of instances which arose whereby interracial neighboring led white women to call into question their stereotyped perceptions of blacks. This type of reaction was reflected in the words of a number of white respondents. One woman phrased her "discovery" this way:

We [she and her husband] didn't like it when they started coming to the project.

71

We felt they ought to stay to themselves. But [since then] I've met some Negroes that are every bit as good as you and me and they deserve a place just like us.

Another white housewife reported:

Every person has got the right to a home, I don't care who it is. They're [blacks] people just like us; some here are better than a lot of white folks. My neighbor is a girl I could be good neighbors with. She's quiet and respectable.

These and other similar changes in racial outlook were reported by white women who also indicated that they had held initially negative feelings toward black neighbors and racial desegregation. The majority of these respondents were life-long border state residents who had never shared a neighborhood with blacks, and many had had few extended contacts with blacks before entering public housing. These women had shared commonly held racial stereotypes but infrequently had been in the position of defending them due to their past experiences.

Unexpected Findings

There were essentially two unanticipated results for the white respondents. The first of these pertains to the hypothesized relationship between duration of residence in the desegregated project and racial tolerance. Whereas the descrepancy between the hypothesis and the results was not as great for the white respondents as it was for the blacks, nonetheless it could not be argued that length of residence in a desegregated environment was positively associated with racial tolerance. One set of conditions that contributed to this finding was the same as that which we argued affected the black housewives, that is, the growing frustrations of project life over time.

In addition to these frustrations, many long-term white residents in the desegregated project harbored a resentment concerning the "Negro invasion" of their project, especially when they witnessed no similar desegregation process in the "Negro projects." White tenants had little financial resources, and satisfactory residential alternatives to public housing were nil. Many of them were alienated from the Housing Authority, and few, if any, felt they could influence its policies. Under the circumstances, a number of the women who resided in the project at the time blacks first moved in and shortly thereafter viewed racial desegregation in their project as an additional and unavoidable indignity. Given their inability to resist the desegregation process, some of these women allowed their feelings of frustration to reinforce or increase their existent racial fears and prejudices. One housewife's comment was typical of this type of resentment:

I don't think it's right and never will. They shouldn't have done it. It causes too much hurt to lots of whites. I don't think there should be this mixing in; it wasn't meant to be. You can't trust them. Since it [desegregation] started, I always keep my door locked.

The second finding for white respondents which was somewhat inconsistent with expectations concerned those housewives who neighbored with blacks. These women were slightly more tolerant of interpersonal relationships with blacks than they were of living in a desegregated neighborhood. Similar results have been found in other research settings,[2] where a comparative lack of tolerance for residential desegregation was attributed to the irrational fear that the value of the neighborhood would deteriorate upon the entry of black families of similar economic means. Although not property owners with an economic investment in the neighborhood, many of the "tolerant" white housewives did express the fear that *large* numbers of blacks might "downgrade" the projects further. They frequently stated their fear that large-scale desegregation would result in sexual relations between black and white adolescents. One white described her concern this way:

I don't like *so many* moving in. They deserve a home too, but don't you think they are going to run down this project? Their bad morals rubs off on the kids. I tell mine to be nice to them, but only to play with them if there are no whites around. I tell them not to mix too much; it's not right. They [black and white children of opposite sexes] are starting hand-holding and kissing already, and that's the beginning of trouble.

Nevertheless, these same women did not view their neighboring or other informal relations with black female adults as threatening. They were more tolerant of residential desegregation than they were of interpersonal-physical contacts with blacks, or of seeing blacks assume influential community positions. Their perception of residing in a desegregated neighborhood could best be described as ambivalent. They did not object to interracial contacts, but they were fearful of the implications of extensive desegreation — implications largely based upon retained stereotypes and the belief that those particular blacks they chose to relate to were somehow exceptionally "acceptable."

The Tenant Selectivity Issue

Before we discuss additional implications of the Border City study, it is appropriate to explore the possibility that a process of differential selection operated to distribute residents in the projects according to their initial racial attitudes. In any study which uses an ex post facto design and views attitude change as a result of interracial contact, the question arises as to what degree initially tolerant attitudes were responsible for one group of respondents entering a racially desegregated environment. In an appendix to their study of interracial public housing, Deutsch and Collins claimed they found little evidence to suggest that differential selection among white residents existed;[3] i.e., tenants in desegregated projects were no less prejudiced initially than those in segregated projects. Their position relied upon three interrelated arguments: (1) lower-income families were so in need of adequate housing that they could not afford to be selective on the basis of racial attitudes; (2) highly intolerant individuals would be no more inclined to move into a segregated project in a black neighborhood than to move into a desegregated project; and (3) racially tolerant responses were higher in desegregated projects regardless of whether or not tenants expected to live with blacks when they applied for public housing.

We feel that differential resident selection no more adequately explains the findings presented here than it did in the Deutsch and Collins research. In the Border City projects, virtually no white applicant was unaware of the pervasively desegregated environment. Whereas this could have conceivably deterred the highly intolerant from applying, we do know that residents voiced similar reservations about moving into public housing whether they entered segregated or desegregated projects. Equal proportions (20-25 percent) of residents entering the segregated and desegregated projects were disturbed about the desegregation issue. Racial desegregation or impending desegregation, however, was not the most offensive aspect of public housing to either group of respondents. Families moved into the Border City because of need and a lack of suitable alternatives. Many of the whites in the John Harrison (desegregated) project entered while it was still a "white project." Newcomers in this desegregated project reported no more interracial neighboring than those who were there prior to or during the initial influx of black families. Reference to table 4-5 suggests this,[a] and it is further confirmed by an examination of the recorded interviews with residents.

As mentioned above, the majority of white respondents grew up in a border state in rural and small town setting where they had comparatively few contacts or associations with blacks. None had lived in truly desegregated neighborhoods prior to entering public housing. They came sharing commonplace black stereotypes, but they had not been raised in Deep South states and exposed to their biracial etiquette. This was true of white residents who entered both segregated and desegregated projects.

Again, unlike the Deutsch and Collins study and those in its tradition, it is not residential occupancy pattern that is viewed as the determinant of racial attitude change; it is both neighboring and other previous equal-status interracial contacts. Whereas those who had previous contacts were somewhat more likely to engage in interracial neighboring, housewives who had such previous contacts were not found disproportionately in the desegregated housing projects.

---

[a]Examination of that table indicates that the overall relationship is a product of the long-term residents' intolerance and not primarily the newcomers' tolerance.

Conclusion

The primary purpose of the Border City research was to explore the contact hypothesis within a different research setting wherein equal emphasis was given to the reactions of black and white respondents. The focus was upon the actual behavior and perceptions of interracial experiences within a situational context of public housing that was undergoing extensive racially desegregation. Unlike previous studies of interracial public housing, no significant relationship existed between desegregated occupancy pattern itself and tolerant racial attitudes. A decade ago, Cook perceptively suggested that researchers interested in studying the effects of intergroup contact should distinguish between the nature of the contact situation and the characteristics of the interpersonal interaction which transpires therein.[4] The context of contact has been described in some detail, especially from the tenants' perspective. And, in addition, the meaning and effect of interracial contacts have been examined from the perspective of both white and black residents.

The institutional and social-psychological context of public housing in Border City included a number of factors which, according to current theory, approximated those likely to exacerbate or reinforce racial disharmony and intolerance. Among the most salient of these factors which hampered the development of congenial relations between the races were: the considerable disruptive and delinquent behavior within the projects, a general lack of any human relations concern on the part of the Housing Authority for the tenants, a large and rapid influx of black families into a formerly segregated white project, and a tenant population which lacked firm grounds for personal security and was, therefore, prone to scapegoat.

Despite the unfavorable and unstable circumstances which existed in the housing community studied and the racial tensions and fears that were shared by many of its residents, there was also an underlying realization on the part of a sizeable proportion of black and white housewives that neither was totally alien to the other. Comments made by respondents of both races indicated that they were aware of certain shared predicaments in their lives. It appeared that the very frustrations of project life that aggravated interracial tensions for some helped reduce intolerance in others. That there was some basis for increased interracial understanding to be derived from the common indignities which black and white respondents felt was reflected in a comment made by one white respondent: "We're in it together. After all, we're all just poor folks."

In terms of the character of the interpersonal interaction which takes place in equal-status situations, we have suggested the reactions to and the effect of the contacts can be quite different for blacks and whites. Recently it has become increasingly clear that the scope of social science research needs to be effectively expanded into the life experiences and perspectives of low-income persons. This is particularly true of the need to better understand the reactions of blacks to interracial contact. Additional research is required to better define how it is that blacks view contact with whites and what kinds of contacts, if any, are viewed as equalitarian from their perspective.[b] As Williams has suggested,[5] and as this study shows, the contact interrelationship can be meaningfully cast in a cost and reward framework. Persons enter into interpersonal exchanges with certain expectations of what they deserve. It was apparently the condescension communicated to black housewives (cost) in contacts with white neighbors which many blacks felt they did not deserve from their white status peers. It was this perception on the part of black housewives which interfered with the expected relationship between contact and increased interracial intolerance.

Nevertheless, as we indicated above, interviews with blacks as well as whites revealed that some residents were aware of certain factors that transcended racial differences. In his discussion of a slum neighborhood as a territory within which different groups manage their co-existence, Suttles writes, "People who routinely occupy the same place must either develop a moral order that includes all present or fall into conflict."[6] Nothing approaching transracial solidarity could be said to have existed in the desegregated project, and, under the circumstances, it would have been surprising if it occurred while the "Negro invasion" continued. However, there was clearly sentiment found among many housewives that black and white women alike were sharing a similar lifestyle within the projects.

Desegregated public housing in Border City was neither characterized by racial harmony nor open racial hostility. There were decided undercurrents of interracial tension, distrust, and resentment. There were also indications of rudimentary interracial understanding and empathy. Housewives in interracial housing could be said to have managed their daily lives, including interracial associations. Neither the white women nor black women were spokesmen for any particular racial view or social order. Whites could not be said to have been caught up in a "backlash" psychology. Blacks were not nationalists, militants, or separatists. These were low-income housewives beset by poverty and a semi-institutionalized environment. And, despite our emphasis upon the black response, it was not unique in many respects. Racial apprehensions kept blacks and whites apart far more than lifestyle differences.

In the study of race relations we have become increasingly interested in conflict and institutional analyses. We have given emphasis to the study of urban racial rebellion, police brutality, black militant groups and the instruments with which the private sector and government agencies perpetuate racial discrimination. Little emphasis, in contrast, has been placed upon the creation and resolution of racial conflicts and tensions in the everyday life experiences of

---

[b]At this point, the reader should be reminded that in our analysis of the black response we have purposely emphasized those findings which deviated from the research hypothesis. Recall that previous equal-status interracial contacts were related to more tolerant interracial attitudes for black respondents. This reinforces the view that the *quality* of interpersonal contacts *within public housing* was not very conducive to increased racial tolerance of whites.

individuals within the community setting. Social change is generally met by a measure of resistance and/or ambivalence. This certainly can be said of race relations. Hesslink argues that the "dispossessed" (e.g., public housing residents) are those who have the least interest in, and certainly the least capability of preserving the status-quo.[7] Whereas rapid, revolutionary change is unlikely to stem from the apolitical or occasionally political lower income groups, it is these individuals who react and adjust their lives in response to community transitions. In the immediate future it is likely to be lower class whites and blacks, for example, who will most likely reside in desegregated neighborhoods. It is possible that in spite of early apprehensions, sharing a neighborhood may eventually result in some measure of interracial cooperation deriving from the recognition of a common plight.

This kind of reaction would appear to be more likely among groups of blacks and whites who share neighborhoods characterized by more favorable circumstances than those found in the Border City projects, although it also appears that commonly held frustrations may also enhance interracial understanding. Such an increase in tolerance should more readily occur among lower-income whites and blacks in communities in which racial polarization has not taken place – notably outside certain large cities in the urban North and in the Deep South. It certainly seems that more favorable relations between the races in public housing would be more likely in projects characterized by greater residential stability and where minority group families did not become the numerical majority within a short period of time. Studies conducted within stable desegregated projects would be able to more successfully isolate the dynamics of interracial behavior.

Additional studies conducted within the context of desegregated public housing should be profitable as compliance with requirements prohibiting intentional racial segregation continues. A larger sample could be drawn from cities and towns of various sizes located in a number of regions.[c] Given sufficient cooperation from local housing authorities, future studies investigating the effects of desegregation and interracial contact on residents' attitudes should be designed to secure measures of individuals' attitudes prior to moving to the projects as well as after they enter. Research on the effects of interracial contact using before-and-after designs is necessary in order to provide more conclusive data on attitudes change. Extensive participant observation techniques should be employed before creating interview schedules and continued during the interviewing in order to complement data collected in formal interviews, serve as a check on interview data, and sensitize researchers to some of the more subtle implications of interracial contact.

---

[c]Although many of us think of public housing as a phenomenon found within the central cities of our largest metropolitan areas, there were 2156 public-housing projects in the United States in 1970. Only 296 of these contained more than 500 apartments. The majority of low-income municipal housing projects are located in medium and small sized cities. Joseph P. Fried, *Housing Crisis U.S.A.* (New York: Praeger Publishers, 1971), p. 72. A substantial number of these projects, especially those located outside the South, contain both white and minority-group residents.

In conclusion, all the normal cautions should be exercised in drawing general inferences from this study. The results are based upon a sample drawn from public housing in a single border state city, and consequently they are open to all the limitations of case studies and of research employing ex post facto designs. Nonetheless, while it is clear that the contact hypothesis is a very useful guide for research, it is an oversimplified theoretical proposition which deserves further specification. The Border City research does not negate the contact hypothesis. It supports the applicability of the contact hypothesis to the racial attitudes of lower-income whites, reaffirms the necessity for careful description of the specific conditions under which such contacts are related to interracial perspectives, and suggests that studies of black reactions to interracial contact are necessary in order to improve our current understanding of race relations.

Notes

Chapter 1
The Contact Hypothesis

1. Samuel A. Stouffer, et al., *The American Soldier Studies in Social Psychology in World War II* (Princeton: Princeton University Press, 1949), vol. 1.

2. Robin M. Williams, Jr., *Strangers Next Door: Ethnic Relations in American Communities* (Englewood Cliffs, New Jersey: Prentice-Hall, 1964).

3. Harold W. Kelley, et al., "Two Functions of Reference Groups," in Harold Proshansky and Bernard Seidenberg, (eds.) *Basic Studies in Social Psychology* (New York: Holt, Rhinehart, & Winston, 1965), p. 314.

4. George E. Simpson and J. Milton Yinger, "The Sociology of Race and Ethnic Relations," in Robert K. Merton, Leonard Broom, and Leonard S. Cottrell, Jr. (eds.), *Sociology Today: Problems and Prospects* (New York: Basic Books, 1959), pp. 397-99.

5. John Dollard, *Caste and Class in A Southern Town* (New Haven: Yale University Press, 1937).

6. Williams, *Strangers Next Door:* pp. *143-222.*

7. Thomas F. Pettigrew, "Racially Separate or Together?" *Journal of Social Issues,* 25 (1969), pp. 54-57.

8. Gordon W. Allport, "Prejudice: A Problem in Psychological and Social Causation," in Talcott Parsons and Edward Shils (eds.) *Toward a General Theory of Action* (New York: Harper Torchbacks, 1962).

9. Earl Raab and Seymour M. Lipset, *Prejudice and Society* (Anti-De-famation League of B'nai B'rith, 1959), p. 22.

10. Arnold M. Rose, "Intergroup Relations vs. Prejudice," *Social Problems,* 4, no. 2 (1956), p. 173.

11. Gunnar Myrdal, *An American Dilemma* (New York: McGraw-Hill, 1964), pp. 75-76. See also Allison Davis, "Acculturation in Schools," in Milton L. Barron (ed.) *American Minorities* (New York: Alfred Kropf, Inc., 1957), p. 446.

12. Frank R. Westie, "Race and Ethnic Relations," in R. E. L. Farris (ed.) *Handbook of Modern Sociology* (Chicago: Rand McNally, 1964), pp. 379-81.

13. Ibid., pp. 581-84.

14. Williams, *Strangers Next Door* pp. 200-01.

15. Morton Grozdins, *The Metropolitan Area as A Racial Problem* (Pittsburgh: University of Pittsburgh Press, 1958). See also, Otis D. Duncan and Beverley Duncan, "Residential Distribution and Occupational Stratification," *American Journal of Sociology* 60 (1955), pp. 493-503; and Leonard Broom and Jack P. Gibbs, "Social Differentiation and Stratus Interrelations," *American Sociological Review* 29 (1964), pp. 258-65.

16. Earl E. Taueber and Alma F. Taueber, *Negroes in Cities: Residential Segregation and Neighborhood Change* (Chicago: Aldine Publishing Company, 1965), p. 1.

17. Charles Tilly, et al., *Race and Residence in Wilmington, Delaware*, (New York: Columbia University Press, 1965), p. 38.

18. Morton Deutsch and Mary E. Collins, *Interracial Housing: A Psychological Evaluation of A Social Experiment* (Minneapolis: University of Minnesota Press, 1951).

19. Ibid., pp. 122-23.

20. Leon Festinger, et al., *Social Pressures in Informal Groups: A Study of Human Factors in Housing* (New York: Harper and Row, 1950).

21. Daniel M. Wilner, et al., "Residential Proximity and Intergroup Relations in Public Housing Projects," *Journal of Social Issues* 8, no. 1 (1952), pp. 45-69.

22. Bernard Meer and Edward Freedman, "The Impact of Negro Neighbors on White Home Owners," *Social Forces* 45 (1965), pp. 11-19. See also, Williams, *Strangers Next Door*; also, Chester L. Hunt, "Private Integrated Housing in A Medium Size Northern City," *Social Problems* 7 (1959-60), pp. 195-209; and, Arnold Rose, et al., "Neighborhood Reactions to Isolated Negro Residents: An Alternative to Invasion and Succession," *American Sociological Review* 18 (1953), pp. 497-507.

23. Meer and Freedman, "Negro Neighbors."

24. Musafer Sherif, "Reference Groups in Human Relations," in Lewis Coser and Bernard Rosenberg, (eds.), *Sociological Theory* (New York: MacMillan Company, 1957), p. 272.

25. Robert W. Greenfield, "Factors Associated with Attitudes Toward Desegregation in A Florida Residential Suburb," *Social Forces* 40 (1961), pp. 31-42.

26. Hunt, "Private Integrated Housing." See also, Kelley, et al., "Reference Groups"; also, Deutsch and Collins, *Interracial Housing*; and, Richard T. Morris and Vincent Jeffries, "Violence Next Door," *Social Forces* 46 (1968), pp. 353-58.

27. Marie Jahoda and Patricia S. West, "Race Relations in Public Housing," *Journal of Social Issues* 7 (1951), pp. 132-39.

28. Festinger, et al., *Social Pressures*, pp. 90-91. See also Williams, *Strangers Next Door*, p. 204; also, Rose, et al., "Intergroup Relations"; and I. N. Brophy, "The Luxury of Anti-Negro Prejudice," *Public Opinion Quarterly* 9 (1945), pp. 456-66.

29. Hunt, "Private Integrated Housing", p. 204.

30. Joshua A. Fishman, "Some Social and Psychological Determinants of Intergroup Relations in Changing Neighborhoods: An Introduction to the Bridgeview Study," *Social Forces* 40 (1961), p. 46.

31. Meer and Freedman, "Negro Neighbors." See also, Rose, et al., "Intergroup Relations."

32. Meer and Freedman, "Negro Neighbors."

33. John Harding and R. Hogrefe, "Attitudes of White Department Store Employees Toward Negro Co-workers," *Journal of Social Issues* 8 (1952), pp. 18-28. See also, D. Katz, "The Functional Approach to the Study of Attitudes," *Public Opinion Quarterly*, 24 (1960), pp. 163-204.

34. Sherif, "Reference Groups." See also, Tamotsu Shibutani, "Reference Groups and Social Control," in Arnold M. Rose (eds.), *Human Behavior and Social Processes* (Boston: Houghton Mifflin Company, 1962); also, Robert K. Merton, *Social Theory and Social Structure* (Glencoe, Illinois: Free Press, 1957), chapters 8 and 9; and Harold H. Kelley, "Two Functions of Reference Groups," in Harold Proshansky and Bernard Seidenberg (eds.) *Basic Studies in Social Psychology* (New York: Holt, Rinehart and Winston, 1965), pp. 210-14.

35. Ralph H. Turner, "Reference Groups of Future Oriented Men," *Social Forces* 34 (1955), p. 131.

36. W. W. Charters and Theodore M. Newcomb, "Some Attitudinal Effects of Experimentally Increased Salience of A Membership Group," in E. E. Hartley, E. E. Macoby and T. M. Newcomb (eds.), *Readings in Social Psychology* (New York: Holt, Rhinehart, and Winston, 1958), p. 276. See also, Merton, *Sociology Today*, pp. 326-30; and Festinger, *Social Pressures*, pp. 76-77.

37. Alberta E. Siegel and Sidney Siegel, "Reference Groups, Membership Groups and Attitude Change," *Journal of Abnormal and Social Psychology* 55 (1957), pp. 360-64.

38. Deutsch and Collins, *Interracial Housing*. See also, Wilner, et al., "Residential Proximity."

39. U.S. Public Housing Administration, Housing and Home Finance Agency, Circular, August 27, 1965.

40. Donald L. Noel and Alphonso Pinkney, "Correlates of Prejudice: Some Racial Differences and Similarities," *American Journal of Sociology* 69 (1964), pp. 609-22.

41. Ernest Works, "The Prejudice-Interaction Hypothesis from the Point of View of the Negro Minority Group," *American Journal of Sociology* 67 (1961), pp. 47-52.

42. Deutsch and Collins, *Interracial Housing*.

43. Robin M. Williams, Jr., *The Reduction of Intergroup Tension* (New York: Social Science Research Council Bulletin, 57, 1947), p. 70.

Chapter 2
The Border City Study

1. Data on Border City's population, its size, growth, and racial composition were taken from: U.S. Bureau of the Census, *U.S. Census of the Population, 1970 General Population: Final Report* (Washington, D.C.: GPO, 1971), and comparable volumes for 1960, 1950 and 1940 together with some material supplied by the Border City Planning Commission.

2. Karl E. Taeuber and Alma F. Taeuber, *Negroes in Cities: Residential Segregation and Neighborhood Change* (Chicago: Aldine Publishing Company, 1965), pp. 31, 33-34.

3. Morton Deutsch and Mary E. Collins, *Interracial Housing: A Psychological Evaluation of a Social Experiment* (Minneapolis: University of Minnesota Press, 1951), pp. 159-66.

4. Matching of the interviewer-respondent racial characteristics has been found to reduce response errors. See Herbert Hyman, et al. *Interviewing in Social Research* (Chicago: University of Chicago Press, 1954), pp. 159-70. Also J. Allen Williams, Jr., "Interviewer-Respondent Interaction: A Study of Bias in the Information Interview," *Sociometry* 27 (September 1964), pp. 338-52.

5. See Frank R. Westie, "A Technique for the Measurement of Race Attitudes," *American Sociological Review* 18 (1953), pp. 73-78. An example of the scales' use can be found in: Frank R. Westie, "Negro-White Status Differentials and Social Distance," *American Sociological Review* 17 (1952), pp. 550-58.

6. See Westie, "Measurement of Race Attitudes," p. 75. for further explanation of this substitution. A discussion of the method of judgment and selection of items in the Thurstone method is found in Claire Selltiz, et al., *Research Methods in Social Relations* (New York: Henry Holt and Company, Inc., 1960), pp. 359-62; more detailed discussion, description and scaling logic is found in Allen L. Edwards, *Techniques of Attitude Scale Construction* (New York: Appleton-Century-Crofts, 1957).

7. The scalogram analysis procedure was applied to the items in each of the four scales. Relatively few nonscale types occurred. The computation technique is found in Edwards, *Attitude Scale Construction*, pp. 178-84. The coefficients of reproducibility for Residential, Positional, Physical, and Interpersonal scales were 0.98, 0.96, 0.98, and 0.94 respectively. For analyses using individuals' total racial prejudice as the dependent variable, the respondents were trichotomized.

Chapter 3
Housewives in Public Housing

1. See Joseph P. Fried, *Housing Crisis, U.S.A.* (New York: Praeger Publishers, 1971), p. 71.

2. Ibid., p. 75.

3. Ibid., p. 74. The national median public housing rent in 1970 was $50.

4. S. M. Miller, Pamela Roby and A. A. deVos van Steenwijk, "Creaming the Poor," *Trans-action* 7, no. 8 (1970), pp. 38-45.

5. William Moore, Jr., *The Vertical Ghetto* (New York: Random House, 1969); Lee Rainwater, *Behind Ghetto Walls* (Chicago: Aldine Publishing, 1970).

6. Ibid., pp. 34-35. Unlike Moore's respectables, these Border City project families do not take part in organized groups outside the projects, nor have they voted regularly in recent elections.

Chapter 5
The Black Response

1. We refer specifically to: Morton Deutsch and Mary E. Collins, *Interracial Housing* (Minneapolis: University of Minnesota Press, 1951) and Ernest Works, "The Prejudice-Interaction Hypothesis from the Point of View of the Negro Minority Group," *American Journal of Sociology* 67 (1961), pp. 47-52.

2. Ibid.

3. Robert B. Johnson, "Negro Reactions to Minority Group Status," in Bernard E. Segal (ed.), *Racial and Ethnic Relations* (New York: Thomas Y. Crowell, 1966), pp. 251-70.

4. William Moore, Jr., *The Vertical Ghetto* (New York: Random House, 1969); Lee Rainwater, *Behind Ghetto Walls* (Chicago: Aldine Publishing, 1970).

5. Lewis A. Coser, "The Sociology of Poverty," *Social Problems* 13, no. 2 (Fall 1965), pp. 140-48.

6. For a discussion of how the challenges and frustrations blacks and whites face differ from one another under biracial neighborhood proximity, see: Harvey Molotch, "Racial Integration in a Transitional Community, *American Sociological Review* 34 (December 1969).

Chapter 6
The Situational Approach To Contact:
Further Interpretations and Conclusions

1. Luigi Laurenti, *Property Values and Race* (Berkeley: University of California Press, 1960), p. 57.

2. For example, see: Morton Goldman, et al., "Residential and Personal Social Distance Toward Negroes and Non-Negroes," *Psychological Reports* 10 (1962), pp. 421-22.

3. Morton Deutsch and Mary E. Collins, *Interracial Housing* (Minneapolis: University of Minnesota Press, 1951), pp. 150-55.

4. Stuart W. Cook, "The Systematic Analysis of Socially Significant Events," *Journal of Social Issues* 18, no. 2 (1962).

5. J. Allen Williams, Jr., "Reduction of Tension through Intergroup

Contact," *Pacific Sociological Review* 7, no. 2 (Fall, 1964), p. 88.

6. Gerald Suttles, *The Social Order of The Slum* (Chicago: University of Chicago Press, 1968), p. 7.

7. This position is discussed in general and as it relates to another research setting in: George L. Hesslink, *Black Neighbors* (Indianapolis: Bobbs-Merrill, 1968), pp. 161-79.

Public Housing
Interview Schedule

I'D LIKE TO BEGIN BY HAVING YOU TELL ME A FEW THINGS ABOUT YOURSELF.

1. In what town and state were you born?_____

1/A. What year was that?_____ 1/B. Did you grow up there? Yes____ No___

(If no) Where did you grow up? (town & state)_____

_____

2. When did you move into <u>this</u> apartment? (month & year)_____

3. Have you ever lived in another apartment in the Border City projects?

Yes____ No____

3/A. (If yes) Which apartment? How long did you live there?_____

_____

4. How long did you live in Border City before you came to the projects? (If lived in more than one apartment, refer to length of
time in Border City before entering the first apartment.)

_____Always lived in Border City_____

5. Where did you live in Border City before you moved into the projects? (st. and area)_____

6. How many times have you moved since 1960? (probe if answer vague)___

7. Marital status (check one)   Married: w/husband___ separated____
                                Divorced____
                                Widowed ____
                                Single ____

8. Do you have a full or part time job? No___ Yes: Full time____
                                                     Part time____
                                                     Periodic work____

85

8/A. Where do you work?_____

What do you do there?_____

9. (If married and w/husband) Where does your husband work?_____

What does he do there?_____

(If appropriate) Unable to work____ Unemployed____ Retired____
Seasonal or periodic work____

10. What was the last year (grade) of school you completed?_____

11. (If married) What was the last year of school your husband

completed?_____ Don't know_____

12. How many children do you have?_____None_____

12/A. Could you tell me how old your children are who live here with you?

Boys___: ___: ___: ___. Girls___: ___: ___: ___. None in project___

13. Compared to the last home you lived in, outside the projects, do you

like this apartment Better___; About the same___; Less_____

(comment:)_____

_____

14. What is the one thing you like most about living here in the pro-

ject? (The neighborhood not the apt.)_____

_____

14/A. What is the one thing you dislike most about living here?_____

_____

_____

15. Why did you move from the last place you lived into the projects? (probe)_____

_____

16. Did you and your family have any trouble getting an apartment here in the projects? Yes_____ No_____

    (comment:)_____

    _____

17. Would you like to continue living here or would you like to move someplace else? (comment:)_____

    (check one) Stay: satisfied_____; resigned_____.
                Move: dissatisfied_____; future aspiration_____.

18. Let's imagine that you were able to make <u>one</u> change in this <u>pro-ject</u>, in order to make it a better place for people like you to live; what change would you make? (if not mentioned, why would you change this?)_____

    _____

    _____

19. As far as you know, what are the people like who live here in <u>this</u> project? (probe: what different groups of people live here?)

    _____

    _____

20. If the apartment next to yours became vacant, what sort of neighbors would you like to have?

    _____

    _____

21. There are (no) (Negro)* (white) families in this part of the project. (If not mentioned in question 20) How(would you) (do you)
feel about having (Negro) (white) neighbors? (probe: why do
you feel like that?)

_____

_____

21/A. Do you think there are any advantages in living in the same
neighborhood with (Negro) (white) families?

Yes_____ No_____

(If yes) What?_____

(If SEGREGATED project, SKIP questions 22 - 25)

22. Do the (Negro) (white) persons who live here in the project seem
any different from the other residents?

Yes_____ No_____

(If yes) How are they different?_____

_____

23. Do the (Negroes) (whites) who live here seem any different to you
than those you see outside the project?

Yes_____ No_____

(If yes) How are they different?_____

_____

_____

* Negro, rather than the currently fashionable term "black", was used
to describe project housewives and their families. Neither blacks nor
whites used the term "black" at the time the data were collected, except in a most derogative manner. Even among older teenagers and the
otherwise "informed" in Border City, the use of the label, "black" had
not yet become widespread.

24. Out of every ten families who live in this project, about how many
would you say are (Negroes) (whites)? (3 in ten, 7 in ten, e.g.)

_____

Don't know_____ (comment:)_____

25. Since you've come here to live, have you come to like the idea of
living in the same neighborhood with (Negro) (white) families more
or less than before?

    More_____ Less_____ No change_____ Don't know_____

26. In your opinion, do you think Negro and white families should live
anyplace in the projects, live in separate buildings, or live only
in their 'own' projects?

    Anyplace_____ Separate buildings_____ Separate projects_____

26/A. Why do you think that this is best?_____

_____

27. Before you moved into the projects did you ....

A ...ever live near (Negro) (white) families?	No_____
	 Yes: _____
	     Same building____
	     across st. or next to_____
	     Same block _____
	     Same neighborhood_____
	 (comment:)_____

B ...ever work on a job with (Negroes) (whites)	No_____ Yes_____
(If yes) What were you doing?; What were they doing?	She was_____ _____ They were_____

She holds such a job now?	Yes_____ No_____
C ...husband worked on a job with (Negroes) (whites)?	No_____ Don't know_____ Yes_____ Doesn't apply_____
(If yes) What was he doing?; What were they doing?	He was_____ _____ They were_____
He holds such a job now?	Yes_____ No_____
D ...have any (Negroes) (whites) in your classes when you went to school?	No_____ Yes_____ (comment:)_____
E ...ever have any (Negro) (white) playmates as a child?	No_____ Yes_____ (comment:)_____
F ...ever have any (Negro) (white) friends?	No_____ Yes_____ (comment:)_____
She has such a friend now?	No_____ Yes_____
G ...your husband have any (Negro) (white) friends?	No_____ Yes_____ Don't know_____ Doesn't apply_____

He has such friends now?   No____ Yes____

H...recall any other personal   No____
contacts you have had, that we
haven't mentioned?   Yes____ (Describe)_____

---

28. When you were a child, what did you <u>learn from</u> your parents (guard-
     ians) about how you should act toward (Negro) (white) persons?
     (probe: how learned; taught or by observing)_____

     Can't remember____ Nothing ____

28/A. Do you still think this is good advice (a good policy)?

       Yes: Why?_____

       No: What is it that has changed your mind?_____

---

29. Do you think your feelings about (Negroes) (whites) have become <u>more</u>

     or <u>less</u> favorable since you've moved into <u>this</u> project?

     More favorable____ Less favorable____ No change____ Don't know____

29/A. (If change) What has made you change your mind?_____

---

30. MOST OF US HAVE A PRETTY GOOD IDEA OF HOW SOME GROUPS OF PEOPLE
     FEEL ABOUT CERTAIN THINGS. I'D LIKE YOU TO CONSIDER SOME OF
     THESE GROUPS AND TELL ME HOW YOU THINK <u>THEY</u> FEEL ABOUT HAVING
     NEGROES AND WHITES LIVING IN THE SAME NEIGHBORHOODS.

How do you think your _ _ _ feel about living in the same neighborhood with....?	Wouldn't they mind or would they be against the idea?			Do they all feel alike or do they differ among themselves?		
	WOULDN'T MIND	AGAINST	MIXED	DON'T KNOW	ALIKE	DIFFER	DON'T KNOW
IMMEDIATE FAMILY							
OTHER RELATIVES							
CLOSE FRIENDS							
NEIGHBORS							
WORK ASSOCIATES (if any)							

31. (Do not reconsider, with the respondent, the 'Don't knows.')

	Do you agree with the way your _ _ _ feels about this matter?			Have you ever -- do you ever discuss this with them?	
	DEFINITELY AGREE	UNDECIDED- NOT ENTIRELY	DON'T AGREE	YES	NO
IMMEDIATE FAMILY					
OTHER RELATIVES					
CLOSE FRIENDS					
NEIGHBORS					
WORK ASSOCIATES (if any)					

OTHER persons or groups she may have discussed this with or whose opinions she regards...?

(Comment:)_____

_____

MANY OF US ARE KEPT BUSY AROUND THE HOUSE THESE DAYS, BUT WE'RE ALSO INTERESTED IN SOME OF THE THINGS RESIDENTS DO OUTSIDE THE PROJECTS.

32. Do you belong to or work with any organized groups outside the project? (groups like the PTA, Girl Scouts, Church groups, Red Cross, etc.

 Yes_____   No_____

(If yes) What groups?_____

_____

33. Do you attend church regularly? (probe) Yes_____   No_____

(If yes) Which church do you go to?_____

34. Are you a registered voter? Yes_____   No_____

(If yes) When did you last vote? '66 local & Congressional_____

 '64 Presidential_____   Neither_____

 (comment:)_____

WE'RE INTERESTED IN FINDING OUT HOW HOUSING RESIDENTS MEET OTHERS HERE IN THE PROJECTS.

35. Could you tell me where (which building) the three persons that you know best, in this project, live?

ID	Same Building	Next or Bldg. Opposite	Other Bldg.	Good Friends?	For Integrated: (Negro?) (white?)
1.					
2.					
3.					

35/A. How did you get to meet these people?

 (1)_____.

 (2)_____.

(3)_____.

35/B. How many other women in this project do you know pretty well?_____

35/C. (For integrated project only) Are any of these other women(Negroes)(whites)?

         No_____ Yes: How many?_____ How did you meet them?

_____

_____

36. In general, would you say that the people here in this part of the project are more or less friendly than in the neighborhood where you used to live?

    More_____ Less_____ About same_____ Don't know_____

37. Do you have more friends in Border City (outside the project) or here in the project?

         Outside_____ Inside_____

38.

		For Integrated: are any of them (Negro) (white)?
A About how often do you go and visit with the women here in the project?	Once/day or more___ Ev Couple days___ Ab Once/week____ Less Once/week____ (comment:)	
B About how often do women come here to visit with you?	Once/day or more___ Ev Couple days___ Ab Once/week___ Less Once/week___ (comment:)	

^CDo you ever help any of the women out here by.....?	caring for child____shopping ____ lending____ when they are sick____ other comment_____
^DDo any of the women help you out by....?	caring for child____ shopping ____ lending____ when you are sick____ other comment_____

39. Would you say that this project is a good place, an average place, or a poor place to raise children?

     good____ average____ poor____ no opinion____

     Why? (probe: what effect on children)_____

     _____

(If No children living with respondent or Segregated project, SKIP question 40.)

40. Do (does) your children (child) have any (Negro) (white) playmates or friends here in the project?

                         No____ Yes____ Don't know____

(If No children, SKIP question 41.)

41. Do (does) your children (child) go to school with (Negro) (white) children?

     No____ Yes____ Doesn't Apple____ Don't know____

41/A. (If yes) Do you think this is a good thing? (probe: why or why not?)

     _____

     _____

42. Do you (would you) have any objections to your children playing with (Negro) (white) children their own age?

     No____ Yes____

(If yes) Why?_____

_____

43. What have you told (would you tell) your children about playing
with and being friendly with (Negro) (white) children their own age?
(probe:)_____

Nothing_____

THERE'S JUST ONE MORE THING I'D LIKE YOU TO DO FOR US: WE'RE INTERESTED
IN KNOWING MORE ABOUT THE WAY PEOPLE FEEL ABOUT ASSOCIATING WITH (NEGROES)
(WHITES) IN DIFFERENT SITUATIONS. EVERYONE SEEMS TO HAVE A LITTLE DIFFER-
ENT FEELING ABOUT HOW NEGROES AND WHITES SHOULD ACT TOWARD ONE ANOTHER.

44. I'm going to read some statements to you, and I'd like you to tell
me whether you agree or don't agree with each one I read and how
strongly you feel about this. I will be asking you what you'd be
willing to do in each these cases, if given the choice; in other
words, if it were 'up-to-you.' We'll mostly be talking about the
"average" (Negro) (white) person.

WOULD YOU AGREE (BE WILLING) TO HAVE A (NEGRO) (WHITE)...

	Strongly Agree	Agree	Unde- cided	Dis- agree	Strongly Disagree
live in the same apartment building I live in.					
as a member of a national patriotic organization.					
have her hair set by the same person that does mine.					
as someone to say hello to.					
live in my end of town.					
as a close personal friend.					
live across the street from me.					
live in my town.					
try on clothes at the same store where I buy my clothes.					

	Strongly Agree	Agree	Unde-cided	Dis-agree	Strongly Disagree
swim in the same pool as I do.					
live in my country.					
ride in the same crowded elevator I am in.					

	SA	A	UD	D	SD
as a member of a Red Cross committee in my town.					
live in my neighborhood.					
as a councilman on my city's council.					
as a dinner guest in my home.					
as someone I might see on the street.					
as an acquaintance.					
use the same towel that I use.					
as head of the local community chest drive.					
as President of the United States.					
use lending library books I also borrow.					
as U.S. Congressmen from my district.					
as a person I might often visit with.					

(Thank the respondent for her time and cooperation. If you think it might be reassuring, reemphasize that the information given is confidential.)

INTERVIEWER'S EVALUATION AND COMMENTS:

Housewife's reaction to the interview: Cooperative_____ Tolerant_____
  Resistant_____

Housewife's understanding of the interview content: Good_____
  Adequate_____ Probably misunderstood_____

Housewife's general outlook could be said to be: Content_____
  Resigned_____ Pessimistic_____

Comment, in a few sentences, about the following:

The interview surroundings and the respondent:

The respondent's attitude toward the other race:

About the Author

W. Scott Ford is currently an assistant professor of sociology and a research associate in the Institute for Social Research at Florida State University. He has been teaching courses in race relations, urban sociology, and the community and is closely affiliated with the Interdisciplinary Program in Urban Minority Problems located in the Urban Research Center. His present interests include black families' attitudes toward and reactions to urban renewal and public housing and the changing political and racial orientations of black college students.

Dr. Ford is the author of a number of articles and papers published in sociological journals and presented at professional meetings. He is the coauthor of *Demand for Higher Education* recently published by D. C. Heath.

Dr. Ford received his Ph.D. (1969) in sociology from the University of Kentucky.